Everybody FIGHTS

KIM AND PENN
HOLDERNESS
WITH DR. CHRISTOPHER EDMONSTON

W Publishing Group
An Imprint of Thomas Nelson

Everybody Fights

Published in Nashville, Tennessee, by W Publishing, an imprint of Thomas Nelson.

Thomas Nelson titles may be purchased in bulk for educational, business, fundraising, or sales promotional use. For information, please email SpecialMarkets@ThomasNelson.com.

ISBN 978-0-7852-3575-0 (audiobook)
ISBN 978-0-7852-3574-3 (eBook)
ISBN 978-0-7852-3572-9 (HC)

Library of Congress Cataloging-in-Publication Data

Library of Congress Control Number: 2020947022

Printed in the United States of America

21 22 23 24 25 LSC 10 9 8 7 6 5 4 3 2 1

For Lola and Penn Charles.
Love is at the center of this book,
and your love inspires us.
Love, Mom and Dad

CONTENTS

INTRODUCTION

KIM

I owe my marriage to pigs in a blanket.

One night, when I was working in television news in Orlando, Florida, my boss sent me to cover the opening of a new mega mall. It wasn't glamorous, but at least I knew I wouldn't have to worry about dinner because the press release promised heavy hors d'oeuvres. PSA: If you are trying to get media to attend an event, offer free food. Nothing gets local news reporters to show up like some mini hotdogs and some booze.

As I was stuffing my fourth pig in a blanket into my mouth, I noticed a small crowd gathered around an extremely tall, insanely handsome guy with great hair. Everyone around him was laughing and smiling and hanging on his every word. Mind you, this was a gathering of people whose jobs were to be magnetic on television, so it was no small thing to be the life of this party. Did I mention he was handsome? I didn't introduce myself because I was seeing someone at the time, and besides, Tall Guy was there with his girlfriend. Of course he had a girlfriend. I wiped the mustard off my fingers and figured that was the last I'd see of him.

But then a few months later, I ran into him again. In the middle of the bar I'd gone to with my girlfriend (I'd broken up with my boyfriend) was Tall Handsome Good Hair Guy up onstage. He cleared a spot and starting dancing. He went from the robot down to the worm, then flawlessly contorted himself into a backspin. He ended with a huge flourish, striking a pose on his side. I had made enough bad decisions in men to realize a good one break-dancing right in front of me. The crowd was still cheering when I turned to my friend and said, "That's the man I'm going to marry."

Before I knew it, that tall handsome dude and I were dancing together. It seemed he'd broken up with his girlfriend too. *Score.* It wasn't romantic—there was no swoony eye contact or *Dirty Dancing*–style heat. It was full-on goofy. For every cringe-worthy dance move I had, he matched it and then some. I did the Mrs. Mia Wallace, and he came right back at me with the Vincent Vega. He cast his imaginary fishing pole; I took three steps out for him to hook me. I laughed harder than I had ever laughed before. In those moments, I knew I wanted to feel that way forever.

We talked and exchanged numbers. You guys, we had "home phones" back then. He called me on a phone that had a *dial tone.* For weeks, every single night after our newscasts we went home and called each other and talked until the wee hours of the morning. I'd never had so much fun talking on the phone. The conversation flowed like we'd known each other forever.

Finally, nervously, we decided we should go on an actual date—in person. I spent hours picking the right outfit so that I could hit that perfect "Oh, this? I just threw this on" look. He picked me up and the first thing he did was hand me a cassette tape. I coolly accepted it with a smile, but my brain was yelling, "He made you a mixtape. Marry this man immediately!"

That evening ended with a monster make-out session and total confidence that this was my person. After only a few weeks of dating, we had the "you're-the-one" conversation. It went like this:

Penn: I think this is it, right?
Kim: Yeah, you're it.
Penn: Cool.
Kim: Cool.

It was just easy. About nine months after that, with sweaty hands and a voice cracking with nerves, Penn asked me to marry him.

During our engagement, I'd occasionally run into a well-intentioned couple who would warn me, "Marriage is a lot of work." I would nod sympathetically, but inside I'd be thinking, *Those poor people. They must not have a solid relationship like we do. I picked the right person. We love each other so much. How could this ever be work?*

You can laugh now. If you need to put down this book to wipe the tears from your eyes, I'll understand.

PENN

Before Kim, I was guilty of what they call serial monogamy. I'd date someone I liked but didn't love and then immediately become exclusive. I'd stay with that mate for well over a year, which was often well past the expiration date. I craved the companionship and intimacy, but I didn't want to get too serious.

This pattern resulted in a lot of breakup conversations like this:

Girl: Penn, I really like you.

Penn: I really like you too.

Girl: But we seem to be in about the same place as we were a year ago.

Penn: You're right! *(pause)* What's wrong with that?

Girl: I think we should break up.

Penn: Okay!

Then along came Kim. She remembers me break-dancing at a nightclub, but I remember meeting her a year earlier than that.

Back when I was a local sports reporter in Florida, I worked Florida Gators football games on the weekends. Not only did I put on a coat and tie to deliver the news from behind a desk, I also had to film the action on the field. I would be on the sidelines of big-time national TV games (which I loved), running up and down the field toting a twenty-pound camera to get coverage. It was a serious workout, and I ended every game soaked in sweat.

One night when the Gators were playing Tennessee, I was hoofing it down the sideline to get to my next location when Kim walked by me. She had her hair down—it was darker than it is now—and she was holding a microphone, wearing jeans and a black leather jacket. She looked annoyed and walked straight past me without looking around. I almost dropped my camera. I thought to myself, *Wow, that is the best-looking woman I've ever seen. And I bet I will never see her again.*

And I didn't.

Until one year later, in the FOX Orlando newsroom. I was looking up at the long bank of TVs nearby that showed our competitors' newscasts. As a sports anchor, I didn't go on the air until the very end of the hour, so it was my job to watch what the other stations were leading with. In the middle TV screen, I saw that face again. This time her hair was pulled back, she was wearing a suit, and she was bathed in the bright light of a live shot, but I immediately knew it was her.

I turned up the volume and heard her voice. It's funny: Kim doesn't love her voice, but I think it's one of her best attributes. It is lower than some female voices, but in a cool, sultry way. My heart started racing. I couldn't believe it. She lived in my town.

About a week later, I went to that media event in search of free food, and we started down the path together. Kim broke my breakup mold. I didn't want to break up with her after a year. I didn't want to break up with her *ever*.

• • •

Cute story, right? But that, of course, was just the beginning. So much goes down in a shared life after the heart-pounding early days. As you might expect, over the next decade and a half as a couple, we went through changes big and small. For example, Kim used to have a "going out tops" section in her closet, max price eight dollars, dental floss shoulder straps, cropped above the navel. Now that section consists of flannel, flannel, turtlenecks, ironic Target T-shirts, and more flannel. In the time it took for her to make that transition, we moved a few times, threw a couple of kids in the mix, and started our own company. It hasn't been an entirely smooth ride. We still love each other, but when your kids act out, your parents get sick, and/or your dog pees on the carpet, we've learned it gets harder to *like* someone. Suffice to say, it's a lot to ask of marriage to be constantly attracted to and in sync with another human.

The upshot was that we fought all the freaking time—and not

just little "Can you please take out the trash?" fights. Fights that reduced us to middle school drama–level simpering messes. Every couple has the kind of fights that go from zero to fantasizing about dialing a divorce lawyer in 0.0 seconds. They leave you feeling cold, resentful, and terribly alone. We had them all the time.

The two of us have been married now for more than fifteen years. Maybe you've seen our videos online—we're the fools who put on matching Christmas jammies, went viral, and then launched a full-time business turning out song parodies that (we hope) bring a smile to your face.

You may very well have come away with the impression that we don't have that kind of fight, that we are always in harmony with each other, and that the worst arguments we have end with Kim giving Penn an indulgent "Oh, *you*!" look. Now it's our turn to laugh. A few years ago, we started noticing comments on our videos that said things like "What a perfect couple!" or "#couplegoals," and we thought, *Who* us? *These people want to be more like* us?

Those videos *are* us, but they are us *plus*, us enhanced, us with the benefit of a suite of editing software, rehearsals, and carefully written scripts. In between singing, dancing, and goofing around, there are countless moments where we shoot lasers out of our eyes at each other, willing the other person to be instantly rendered mute.

Having a healthy marriage means learning how to disagree without it leading to a breakdown every time. Like when we were all sheltering in place during the COVID-19 pandemic. We saw so many posts of people pulling their hair out as they tried to figure out how to spend 24/7 with their spouses. Although we were struggling with sadness and confusion along with everyone else, we had a jump on the all-day-every-day-no-break-from-each-other-ever marriage. For the past five years, we have worked together out of our home. We talk to each other easily seven hours a day. Six of those hours are debates about what rhymes best with *booty* or how to get a camera angle that doesn't take Penn's chin from a double to a triple, but the last hour of our day is us talking about our relationship. As the whole world has learned, disagreements are inevitable when you spend that much time with someone, and if we had a knock-down, drag-out fight every time we saw things differently, we would never accomplish anything. So we've made it a priority to put in the work required for a healthy marriage, and here's why.

You know how when you get a new car, it's perfect? It looks good. It smells good. It makes you feel good about yourself. But after a bit of use, even the best car starts having issues, and you need to take it in for a little maintenance—an oil change, brake pad replacements, new tires. Maybe the A/C is making a weird noise like there's a dead rat stuck in there. It's still a great car; it just needs care to keep it from exploding into a glorious fireball.

When we notice something going wrong with a car, we take it in to the shop. We drink terrible coffee and wait in a filthy room for two hours because that's what it takes to fix whatever is wrong. We do the work because we know that ignoring a problem could lead to bigger troubles down the road. Our question for you is—why don't we do that kind of maintenance on our marriages? Surely our marriages are as important as our cars, aren't they?

Not one single marriage in the history of marriages has run perfectly all the time. We have fights, but we just keep driving down the road. Philosophical differences grow over time, but we figure out ways to avoid them, and we just keep driving down the road. Intimacy issues crack open, but we keep driving down the road. As long as things don't break down completely, we keep driving down the road.

Is it our pride that makes us terrified to admit our marriage needs a tune-up? Are we afraid that when we take it in, someone will open up the hood and say, "Oh, man, you have *a lot* more problems than you thought! That'll be $4,264"?

This is *marriage* we're talking about, our most sustained and sustaining relationship with a person who we promised to love and support as long as we both shall live. Shouldn't we look at the 55 percent divorce rate and say, "Forget pride—what do I need to do to take care of this thing"?

At our worst, when our fights reached critical mass, we were miserable. We knew there had to be a better way to keep our marriage running smoothly, so we found ourselves an honest mechanic—our lifelong friend Dr. Christopher Edmonston. Christopher is the pastor of our church, and, lucky for us, one of his special interests is marriage care—plus, we trust that he won't hose us on repairs. For years now, Christopher has gone under the hood to show us how to tweak the way we communicate with each other so that our marriage is a well-oiled machine. In this book, we will share what we've learned from him and from our years together.

Before we go any further, this part is also important: sometimes marriages get totaled. We know that happens. It happens more than half the time, and it has happened to a lot of people very close to us. If your marriage is teetering on the brink, this book may not be for you. If you are dealing with infidelity or addiction or mental illness or chronic illness or serious trust issues, please feel free to read this book and take from it whatever resonates, but it would be irresponsible of us to pretend to have the background to help you surmount those obstacles. We aren't scientists or therapists or even polyamorists. We try to make people happy by dancing around in our jammies on the internet. We try to make each other happy by communicating clearly and effectively using the techniques Christopher has taught us.

This book is for those of you who are married and want to stay that way. It's for couples who just aren't feeling heard by their partners, who can't break out of their bad patterns of communication. This book gives you strategies that have made our marriage stronger over the years, and we hope they do the same for yours.

Why should you listen to us? After all, most books about improving your marriage are written by someone who has a bunch of letters after their name or a lab named after them. We don't have secondary degrees. We're not performing rigorous double-blind studies on the mating habits of rats; we *are* the rats. We're not decked out in lab coats testing hypotheses; we're in the maze looking at each other like, "I told you we should have gone left." We're going to share what we've learned from the times we've felt helplessly stuck in the maze, and then we'll share the strategies we've discovered that have helped us get out of the darn thing time and again so we can enjoy our lives and each other.

With Christopher's help, we've learned how important it is to confront the topics we want to avoid (*Why aren't we having sex? Who gets to decide how we spend our money? Can you please help out more?*) and how to have conversations that don't dissolve into toxic puddles of conflict sludge.

Our goal has been to make our fights productive. You know how when you rake the yard, if you let the piles of leaves just sit there, the first gust of wind will send them scattering across the grass again? You might as well have not raked in the first place. But if you turn those piles into compost, you can use them to nourish your yard and make your soil richer. We want to teach you how to turn your recurring fights into useful conversations that will help your marriage thrive.

In this book, you'll learn how to

- ask for what you want
- stop hijacking conversations
- use magic words to change course midfight
- tell your partner exactly what they want to hear—without faking it
- declare bankruptcy on perfection
- treat your partner like a stranger—and feel closer than ever as a result
- amend your secret contracts
- banish the three Ds—distraction, denial, and delay
- harness the power of metacommunication
- stop stonewalling

Every technique in this book was forged and battle-tested in our own relationship. We'll go into the gory details—the real masks-off, gruesome, nitty-gritty—of our most stubborn fights. We'll start out with a he said / she said story so you can hear both sides of how we landed deep in the jungle of our stickiest issues, and then we'll come together to pass along the wisdom Christopher gave us that helped us hack our way through and come out the other side feeling closer to each other and better understood.

Rules of War

In a marriage based on respect and love, some behaviors are off the table no matter what. Early on, before we had even met Christopher, we established what we call our *rules of war* to guide us. Our list:

- No name-calling or other insults.
- No swearing.
- No leaving.
- You know how to hurt your partner—don't do it on purpose.

We're going to spend the rest of this book focusing on the do's of good communication, but before we do, take a minute and write your own list of behaviors that are forbidden. You might include rules about your tone, whether you should fight in front of the kids (we do!), or when to call for a time-out.

WHAT'S THE MAGIC WORD?

If there's one thing we've learned under Christopher's guidance, it's that there are no magic bullets—but there *are* magic words. You know how when you were younger and you wanted something so bad it felt like your life would end if you didn't get it immediately? After you had begged and pleaded, your mom would say, "What's the magic word?" and you would spit out "Please?" and *ta-dah*, ice cream. Christopher is a master of coming up with choice phrases and key words that, while they don't solve everything instantaneously, help end your misery because they illuminate a way forward. We use these magic words as beacons to show us a better way. In each chapter, we'll share not just techniques and strategies but also the magic words that have helped us get through fights with the least amount of drama—and even avoid a few in the first place. We can't tell you the number of times Christopher has given us notes on our fights and we've turned to each other and said, "Oh, man, why didn't I say it like that?" or "Well, if you had put it that way, we never would have gotten into that fight in the first place!"

We want to be totally upfront with you right from the start. This whole endeavor—marriage, communication, enduring love and respect—is a work in progress. We have not found a cure for being two different people with two different perspectives and sets of experiences. To be honest, we wouldn't want that—it sounds a little Stepfordy. We cherish our differences. They add a sense of excitement and the promise of growth in our relationship that we would miss if they weren't there. We know that the trade-off is that we will get in another fight soon. In fact, just this morning we were in danger of combusting over whose turn it was to go for a run while the other stayed with the kids. It's a daily practice. But we are armed with the confidence that we will work through it and feel good about the result.

Yes, it takes vigilance and a willingness to try and try again, but loving your person should never be a chore. Those well-meaning people who warned Kim were right—marriage *is* work. But keeping up on the maintenance is worth it.

01

THE BATTLE OF THE BRA

THE FIGHT

PENN

It was Wednesday, and I had had *a week*. We had been so swamped with work that the only time I had left my house was to go see my dad to try to convince him (again) that having my mom live under the same roof with him would be dangerous because they weren't able to take care of each other anymore. That is an argument you should never have to have, but there we were.

On the way home, I called Kim. She was her usual spectacularly empathetic self. She knows how to talk to me when I am having family issues. She was patient, supportive, and loving to a fault. However, I forgot all of that ten minutes later, because after she had soothed my nerves, the rest of the conversation went like this:

Kim: I was thinking chicken and cauliflower rice for dinner?

Penn: *(to self)* May I quote Alexander Hamilton? "Grilled chicken is delicious, but only like once a week." Okay, maybe he didn't say that, but I bet he thought it. There is a limit to how much grilled chicken breast a person can eat, and I have reached mine. I just finished the leftovers at lunch of the chicken leftovers we had for dinner last night, left over from Monday, which is "Chicken Night" at our house. I can't eat chicken again. Please don't make me eat chicken again. Also, cauliflower rice smells like unflushed toilet pee.

Kim: Hello? Are you there?

Penn: Yeah, um, sorry. Hey, honey, how would you feel about going out to dinner tonight? Nothing fancy, just a chance to get out of the house?

Kim: Uhhhhh, I don't know. I just took my bra off.

Penn: Okay, so, just put it back on and we'll leave in ten minutes. *(to self)* Problem solved.

Kim: *(silence)*

Penn: Kim?

Kim: I don't think you understand what I said. *I just took my bra off.*

Penn: So?

Kim: What about the dinner I'm making? Do you think I am cooking this food for fun?

Penn: No, that's why I thought maybe we could go get something different.

Kim: So you don't like my cooking? I would be happy to let *you* cook anytime if I didn't fear it would all end up down the disposal.

Penn: Maybe if you didn't always make me cook mung beans and lentil pasta, my cooking would taste a little better.

Kim: I'm keeping us healthy, and if I didn't plan the meals, who would?

Penn: You always want to plan everything. Can't you be a little spontaneous?

Kim: Oh, and throw away our money on restaurant meals?

Penn: I just thought it would be easier.

Kim: If you would pitch in, things *would* be easier. I'm the only one who ever does anything around the house. Do you think food magically appears in the fridge?

Penn: I took both kids to their doctors' appointments last week, *and* I did everything on that list you gave me last weekend.

Kim: That's another thing. Why can you never see what needs to be done on your own? Why do I always have to do everything? How selfish can you be?

KIM

That is not at all what happened. First of all, it was chicken *thighs*, not chicken breast. Second, the night before had been turkey chili so, okay, yes, that was from the poultry category, but it was not chicken breast. Totally different.

I'll admit that not all of my meals are Pinterest-worthy, but my family is alive and healthy. Keeping them that way takes *work* even in the best of times, and those were not the best of times. On the night of the Bra Battle, I was spent. We were living in a state of high and constant anxiety over Penn's parents' safety, and I was exhausted. I needed to be in my house, in my twenty-year-old sweatpants, recharging on the couch. Did I want to prepare dinner that night? Of course not. But I had defrosted those bleeping chicken thighs, and we were going to eat them. I just needed to put calories in our bodies. I wasn't trying to impress anyone—and that went double for how I looked. I was in for the night. To wit, I had taken off my bra.

Ladies, back me up on this. The bra might not be the whalebone corset of yore, but it is definitely uncomfortable. I applaud women who feel free enough to go without one in public, but I'm not there yet. The minute I'm done with the day, my hand goes to my back and releases the clasp. That moment signals the end of my commitments to the outside world. Other than making dinner, nothing productive happens after the bra is off. I'm safe. I'm done. The couch awaits.

I get that it sounds ridiculous that I couldn't bring myself to put my bra on again, but hear me out: everything had been, and needed to be, all about Penn for a while. Both of his parents were crashing through the stages of dementia at breakneck speed. Managing the logistics of moving them into the right care centers was the least of it. It was as draining as it was heartbreaking. I had shut down any needs of my own, and I wasn't taking care of myself. I could handle putting most things on hold—the gym, long walks with my closest friends, and so on—but I desperately needed to decompress. When it looked like my chance to unwind was about to evaporate, I lost it. I took that chicken and weaponized it. It might have been less toxic if it had given us salmonella.

BREAK IT DOWN SO YOU DON'T BREAK UP

Does this sound like something that happens in your house? We're guessing yes. We have been struck by how much commonality there is among the fights couples have. The details might be different—instead of scrapping over dinner, it might be a tiff over who paid which bill or whether one partner works too much or which car to buy—but the patterns (communication short circuits, escalation, and hurt feelings) are remarkably similar across the board.

We fight a lot. Like, *a lot*. More than your average couple on a sitcom. We work together from the home that we live in and parent in together, so things come up. Couple things, coworker things, parent things—some days, it feels like *everything*. We have more than accumulated our ten thousand hours of fighting, which we're pretty sure Malcolm Gladwell would say puts us in the expert category. It may seem strange to boast about, but we have gotten pretty dang good at it. With the help of Christopher, our pastor and marriage coach, we have figured out how to make our fights less destructive.

The golden ticket has been something Christopher introduced us to called *metacommunication*, or talking about *how* we talk to each other. We now make it a practice to Monday morning quarterback our fights. We do a postgame analysis to determine what went right, what went wrong, and which bad habits we need to break so we can do better next time. Christopher has shown us how to pull back to a wide angle so we can see exactly what went down on the field. By examining how we communicate, we've come up with some techniques that have improved our communication and our marriage exponentially.

If you are like us and you find yourself frequently clashing with your partner, we have good news: fights can be productive. They allow you to learn more about yourself and your partner than nearly anything else you do together. You don't learn much about your partner's inner world when you're cooking dinner or watching a *Friends* marathon, but when you clash, you push against each other, and in the process, you learn about boundaries, you learn what vulnerabilities those boundaries are protecting, and you learn what matters to you and what matters to your partner.

In the way that pruning a rosebush isn't bad for the rosebush, conflict isn't bad for a relationship. What's bad is unhealthy, abusive conflict, or conflict that goes to waste because you haven't examined it and learned from it. In a good fight, you don't experience a win or a loss; you experience something new about yourself or your partner. Productive conflict hones, shapes, and refines your relationship. That's why we have gotten so intentional about talking about our fights. We mine them for ways to improve how we talk to each other and to bring us closer together.

In this chapter, we'll use our bra fight to illustrate how to perform a good fight analysis:

- Nail your timing.
- Take a thirty-thousand-foot view.
- Examine *how* you said what you said.
- Stay in the airport.
- Ask yourself, "Did we resolve it?"

After you've gone through the process enough times, you might find, as we have, a new confidence in your ability to work things out. Metacommunication doesn't always work perfectly, but it has radically changed the way we fight and communicate.

NAIL YOUR TIMING

First things first: in order to do a successful postgame analysis, you have to wait for the game to be over, when the sweat has dried and your pulse has returned to normal. Our sympathetic nervous system—our fight, flight, or freeze response—kicks in during times of stress. This system developed when most of the threats we faced were to our physical safety (saber-tooth tiger, jealous caveman with club, snake in the grass), but it activates rapidly and fully in face of contemporary stress (threat to livelihood, damaged ego, relationship in jeopardy). Once the sympathetic nervous system kicks into gear, it puts your body through more changes than puberty in just a few seconds. Your heart rate skyrockets, your blood pressure increases, your pupils dilate to let in more light (the better to see the glint of a saber tooth), your muscles get pumped up because your veins constrict. As an added benefit, you have trouble concentrating on long-term tasks. The sympathetic nervous system is terrific at keeping us from getting mauled by a saber-tooth tiger, but when it comes to explaining to your partner how what they just said hurt your feelings, it is mud.

When your sympathetic nervous system activates, it's like someone has pushed the mute button in your brain. You feel so worked up that you can't find words among all the rage or sadness or shame clamoring in your skull. Actually, that is a pretty good description of what happens on a cognitive level. Some subjects are so touchy, so likely to flood your brain with stress chemicals, you actually *cannot* talk about them. On an episode of the podcast *On Being with Krista Tippett*, psychiatrist Bessel van der Kolk explained that this happens because the Broca area of your brain (which contains the neurons responsible for your speech function) surrenders. Your emotions trample all over your ability to put together a coherent sentence. You shout emotional nonsense or get so worked up that you say nothing at all. We say that someone is out of their mind when this happens.

If you find yourself saying things to your partner like "Please be reasonable" or "Can't we talk about this rationally?" when you're fighting, it's useful in those scenarios to remember that it's possible that your partner *can't* speak rationally, at least not at that moment. You can make all the logical arguments you want when someone is upset, but if they are experiencing an overwhelming feeling, especially one linked to a traumatic experience, you are not going to be able to break through. You're just not speaking their language.

Screw You, Sympathetic Nervous System

There are a variety of things you can do to calm your sympathetic nervous system. They aren't going to transform you from Mr. Hyde back into Dr. Jekyll instantaneously, but they should help bring you from a hyperactive 10 down to, say, a more rational 5. On a small piece of paper you can keep in your wallet, write out one or more of the suggestions below and refer to them when you are so worked up that you aren't able to think clearly:

- Take five deep breaths, filling your belly first, then your lungs.
- Listen to [your favorite song].
- Spend one minute imagining [happy place].
- Pet [your pet's name].
- Do three rounds of sun salutations.
- Check in with your body. Place your hands over wherever you are feeling tension and let them rest there.
- Massage your neck and shoulders.

The best time to go over what has gone down in a big blowup is once you feel safe again, when your sympathetic nervous system has reset to its default state. If none of the techniques above is effective for you, your best bet is time. Let some pass, and you will gradually recover your ability to speak and think rationally.

Our bodies are not built to stay in a state of high activation indefinitely. It's simply too stressful. That's why, contrary to a lot of advice we've read, we're comfortable going to bed angry if we are still too agitated to talk through what's eating us before bedtime. We know that the next day the conversation will be more productive if we are well rested and have some distance from the fight than if we try to tackle it while feelings are still running high. As Christopher puts it, you've got to wait until the hottest part of the fire is out before you can worry about rebuilding anything. For some fights, the fire will be out after five minutes; for some it will take a full day. When you've settled, then you can begin to talk things through without your sympathetic nervous system sabotaging you. You've calmed down; there's no shouting. You can sit down and speak to each other like adults.

THIRTY-THOUSAND-FOOT VIEW

When Christopher first said the word *metacommunication* to us, we acted like those kids in grade school who laughed along at the fake "No soap, radio!" joke. We nodded and pretended like we were totally looped in, while secretly thinking, *What?* But thanks to many patient lessons with Christopher, we really do get it now and we want to spread the word. Metacommunication is simply talking about how you and your partner communicate.

(How many of you just googled "No soap, radio" just now? The Wikipedia page is solid, right?)

To be able to talk about your communication habits, you need to be able to see them clearly. In order to do that, you need to change your perspective, which is why step one of good metacommunication is to take a thirty-thousand-foot view. What do we mean by that? Pull back a bit and ask yourself how you felt in your body during the fight. Now pull back a bit more and ask what circumstances you were in. What was the environment like? Now zoom waaaaaay up. What else was going on in your life and heart at the time that may have contributed to the argument?

Seeing Better From Farther Away

Next time you've had a fight and you can't see two feet in front of you because your view is so fogged by emotions, get above the atmosphere and try to take in the whole scene. Once you hit thirty thousand feet, take note of where you were:

- Physically—were you tired, hungry, hot, tipsy?
- Emotionally—were you stressed, already on edge?
- Mentally—where was most of your attention?
- Personally—what aspect of how you were raised might have affected this fight?

Write down your responses and have your partner do the same. Then exchange lists. We promise you'll see things more clearly.

From thirty thousand feet, you can see both people's perspectives equally instead of getting stuck in first-person-shooter perspective, where everything that comes into view is a potential threat. When you pull back to thirty thousand feet, you can remember there are two people involved in this dynamic and the ultimate goal of the fight is to get back in harmony with your partner, not to win.

When we went to thirty thousand feet after the Bra Battle, we could see that when Penn's emotional black hole of dealing with his parents' dementia collided with Kim's storm cloud of exhaustion, we combusted into a supernova of a fight. That context is fair game to discuss when you are analyzing your fight. Take the time to explain to your partner, "I was feeling emotionally overwhelmed, and I wanted to get out of the house to let off some steam" or "I had already clocked out after a long day, and I just didn't have it in me to go out again." Pointing out where you were coming from emotionally can help your partner to see that the fight wasn't about only them—it was also about the six billion other things that go on in a human heart and mind at any given moment. Learning what your partner thought and felt helps you understand why they reacted the way they did. Greater understanding leads to greater intimacy.

PENN

When I take the thirty-thousand-foot view, I can see that sometimes what's upsetting Kim has nothing to do with me. Maybe she's feeling upset about something that happened earlier with a work contact or maybe something she's feeling can be traced back to her parents' divorce. Maybe she was just hungry. In the Bra Battle, I hadn't been able to see and appreciate how exhausted she was until the two of us cooled down and zoomed out to thirty thousand feet. I got a sense of what else was going on that I couldn't see in the moment. I think my ADHD kind of comes in handy when it's time to shift perspective. Not in a way where I say, "Oh, a squirrel! Let's see where he goes!" But more like, "Wait a minute. Whether I eat chicken for dinner (again) does not matter that much. What's important is that over there. My job is more important. My family is more important. Our marriage vows are more important." It helped me to chill out a little and become less defensive when I could see that Kim's reaction wasn't about me.

IT'S NOT WHAT YOU SAID–IT'S HOW YOU SAID IT

Another important thing to look at when you are analyzing your fights is *how* you said what you said. The words you choose, the tone you take, and how your bodies relate to each other in space can have an enormous impact on how your argument unfolds. This Christmas, we're pretty sure Christopher is going to create a pillow for us that says, "It's not what you said—it's how you said it."

Some of our worst fights start not as a result of conflicting values or because we disagree with each other but because the way we express ourselves is pitiful. Before we went through metacommunication boot camp with Christopher, both of us would do the passive-aggressive shoulder shrug: "I guess *I'll* be the one to get up and change her diaper." Or "No, no, don't you worry about the vacuuming. I'll do it." What you said may not technically be offensive, but let's be real: when you say something passive-aggressive, you know how you meant it.

Possibly worse than when we are passive-aggressive is when we jump at hyperspeed to hyperbole. As soon as one partner starts with blanket statements—"You always" or "You never"—you know you are in the danger zone. First of all, nuh uh. No one *always* does anything. This is a failed line of argument from the get-go. Plus, once those accusations start, it's never going to end well. As you're doing an analysis of a fight, keep an eye out for these phrases:

- "You do this all the time."
- "You constantly . . ."
- "You always . . ."
- "You never . . ."

Strike *you* statements from your conversations and replace them with the magic words "I feel . . ." What you say after "I feel" is always true. It's subjective. Plus it doesn't send your partner into a defensive position. It's not an accusation. You're not forcing your opinion on somebody else. You're simply stating how you feel. (We'll revisit the magic of "I feel" in the next chapter.)

We are 1,000 percent positive we could have saved ourselves a lot of anger and hurt feelings if one of us had had the presence of mind to start our sentences with *I feel* instead of *You* during our Bra Battle.

STAY IN THE AIRPORT

When it came to the Bra Battle, we knew we needed to bring in an expert for the assist, so at an appointment with Christopher, we asked him to weigh in. Once we had given him the blow-by-blow, he said, "You see what happened there, right? You started with one fight and then escalated into every fight you've ever had or thought about having."

He was right. We had gone from, "Can't we have something besides chicken?" to "You're selfish" in record time. Every issue that had been bothering us came pouring out, like trash spilling from a slit in an overstuffed garbage bag—and it was rank. Christopher gently chastised us, saying that we had failed to *stay in the airport.*

Oh, do you not know what that means? Don't worry; it took some explaining before we understood it too. But once we got the concept, we never forgot it. The idea is this: when you're trapped in a fight, you can't bounce around all over the place trying to find a way out. We had moved on too quickly to the next issue before we had the first one resolved. Christopher explained that we needed to stay in the airport. It might be a way station where everyone is on edge and feels impatient to get out of there ASAP, but if you run to the ticket counter to change your ticket or make for the rental car station just so you don't have to be there anymore, you are never going to arrive at your destination. You need to stay awhile if you ever want to take off. It's unpleasant, and no one likes it, but the only way out is through.

Ever since Christopher taught us the phrase *stay in the airport* we have used these magic words to remind ourselves to stay put long enough to work through whatever issue we're debating. Staying in the airport is a godsend because you limit yourself to one need, which makes the experience so much less overwhelming. It's not "I need you to address every aspect of our relationship in a single conversation." It's "I'd like to see this one thing through from beginning to end"—a far more reasonable goal.

One sure sign that you've left the airport is when you pivot from something logical and concrete ("What are we having for dinner tonight?") to something emotional ("I want to go out because I feel trapped"). When you leap from the concrete to the abstract, you've raised the stakes considerably. Suddenly, you're in emotional territory where meaning becomes treacherously slippery. During our Bra Battle, once we had pivoted, we started interpreting what the other person said in a way that was heavily influenced by our own insecurities and vulnerabilities. When Penn said that Kim wasn't spontaneous, Kim heard, "I find you boring and uninteresting." When Kim brought up how much they were spending on restaurant meals, Penn heard, "You aren't providing for your family." That's a long way from chicken, and a long way from the original issue of how to reconcile our conflicting needs to get out of the house or hunker down at home.

As you break down where things broke down, take note of those pivot points. They signal that you're dealing with an important topic. It might not be the time to address it—remember, you're staying in the airport to hash out your original issue—but just because you are focused on one thing at a time doesn't mean that the thirty other issues that came up during the fight don't matter. Catalog those to return to in future conversations.

KIM

I am the queen of escalating. Not just in my marriage, but in disagreements with family members, coworkers, and friends. Once I've left the airport, the fight becomes an excuse to say all those things that I don't get to say on a daily basis. I know I'm in trouble when I find myself saying things like, "And furthermore . . ."

I won't lie. The level of restraint required to stay in the airport is huge. The urge to bring up a whole list of other things that happened last week, last month, or last year is strong. But I'm telling you, if you can make yourself stay in the airport, you'll find that your marriage gets exponentially better.

YOU SAY YOU WANT A RESOLUTION

No analysis is complete without looking at the final outcome. How did the fight turn out? What was the upshot? And what can you learn from it? What do you need to practice? What skills can you improve?

When we sit down to review a fight, we have a cup of coffee and try to get to the bottom of what we were trying to convey in the heat of the moment. We'll say, "Okay. You mentioned you really don't like it when I say this." Or, "You said you really would appreciate it if I did X. What does that mean to you?"

From there we try to figure out what's next. We learned that from working in newsrooms. It's always the last question you ask in an interview—what's next? It's not enough to point out the problem; you need to take action and bring what you've learned with you into your next fight.

After our bra fight, Penn relented and ate the dinner he really didn't want to eat, but he was pretty salty about it. It wasn't until the next day when we'd had a chance to talk about where things had gone wrong in our fight, to explain to each other what else was going on in our lives and minds, and to see the whole thirty-thousand-foot picture that we understood both of us had been stressed to the max. Our fight wasn't about dinner; it was about our need to recharge. We agreed that next time we encountered a similar situation, we'd enjoy dinner at home, and then Kim could melt into the couch while Penn met up with friends to watch some sports afterward.

Christopher told us that even couples who are really good at doing breakdowns of their big arguments have a hard time incorporating those lessons into their future behavior, so if you're feeling discouraged after a few attempts, take heart. Things will get better. Once you've practiced, you'll be like an elite athlete whose heart rate goes back to resting quickly because they are so accustomed to the hard work. Lucky for us, we have had thousands of chances to fight. We've gotten good at recovering, and we've even started to incorporate what we've learned into our fights *as we are having them*, which makes the fights easier and far less destructive.

How Was It for You?

Here's a postfight analysis worksheet for you to use after you've had a tough fight. You can fill it out separately and share your answers later or fill it out together as a couple.

- What was the conversation like for you?
- How was our timing?
- What else was going on in our lives that might have contributed to this fight?
- If I'm honest, I can see that this part of my personality, which has nothing to do with you, showed itself during the fight . . .
- I thought you did this well . . .
- How did the fight start?
- Where did we end up?
- Are the two related?
- What were some of the pivot points as we spoke?
- What issues came up? Which of those do we need to have a conversation about?
- How often did we use *you* statements versus *I/we* statements?
- If I could go back to the worst moment of the fight and rewrite what I said, I would say, "I feel . . ."
- What resolution did we come to?
- What can we learn from how we talked to each other?
- What can we do better next time?

When you fight, and you will, the result should be not just a resolution but also a greater understanding of each other and more intimacy. Each conflict should nudge you a bit closer together because you've learned something new about your partner—and you should know yourself a little bit better too.

02

CAN'T YOU JUST BE HAPPY FOR A MINUTE?

THE FIGHT

PENN

I don't like to brag, and I am fully aware that what I'm about to say sounds an awful lot like bragging, but last year, Kim and I made a video that got seventy-five million views in one week. That's like a quarter of America, or all of France, or three of Australia. After it started catching on, nearly every major news outlet called us—I was even interviewed by a reporter from the *Wall Street Journal*. Come on, you would brag too.

The video was a simple close shot of me singing a modern version of the holiday tune "Baby, It's Cold Outside." Kim and I had gotten the idea after there had been a nationwide hullabaloo over whether the song's premise of a guy trying to persuade a woman to stay at his place a little longer was inappropriate. We thought it would be funny to rewrite it from the perspective of a modern dude trying to be as woke as possible. I did my best croon:

"I really can't stay . . ."
"Okay, you're free to go."
"I've got to go away."
"Understood. No means no."

It caught on like wildfire. People from both sides of the "Cold Outside" debate loved it. The liberal side of America thought it showed why the song should be taken off the radio because it highlighted how inappropriate the lyrics were. The conservative side of America thought it was a good way to poke fun at the liberal snowflakes who were way too sensitive.

When I saw how many views we'd racked up, I was ready to run around the quad naked like Will Ferrell in *Old School.* That many views could set the table for the next twelve months, keep us financially stable, and allow us to do all kinds of cool things in the future. Just as important, the video's success was a big affirmation that we had what it took to make it in the line of work that we had decided to pursue.

But that week, to my shock, Kim spent a lot of time crying. She will do a better job explaining why than I could, but the short of it was she just couldn't focus on all those good things, because when a video spreads that widely, there will inevitably be some negativity in the mix. Even though we are talking like only 0.0001 percent negativity, it didn't matter—0.0001 percent of seventy-five million is still a lot more than you might think.

But Kim's inability to see the positive in what I considered an absolute win baffled me. The whole point of making these videos was to create something that people would love and share. I thought, *Look, I know you aren't always super happy, and I don't expect you to be a grinning buffoon, but if there were ever a time to celebrate, this is it! Right here! Right now! Why can't you just be happy?*

KIM

I really was the Grinch who stole Christmas that year. No matter how many views that video got, and no matter how happy Penn was about it, I just couldn't get in the mood to pop some bubbly.

Like many people, for most of my life I hadn't really given "Baby, It's Cold Outside" much thought. To me, it was just part of a cute scene in *Elf* when Zooey Deschanel sang in the shower—until people started calling radio stations and requesting it be taken off the air. *Huh.* I started listening a little more closely to the song lyrics, and while I got that when it was written the intent was just to be flirty, through the lens of current culture, it did seem a little off. And by off, I mean rapey.

So we rewrote the song with an emphasis on consent. Penn put on a wacky suit and we set up the camera and microphone in the living room with no lighting or anything. It was totally bare bones. We recorded him singing in one take. He put some graphics on it that afternoon, and we published it the next morning. Within hours, it was everywhere. We'd gone viral.

This might surprise you, but I do not like it when our videos go viral, and I'll tell you why. On our platforms, the comments are typically very positive and community-building. There's the occasional crack about my dance skills or Penn's outfits, but that's usually as harsh as it gets. But when a video gets tens of millions of views, people go from writing tweets poking fun at my dancing to writing thought pieces and open letters. And in the worst cases, they start attacking one another.

I can handle a little shade thrown at my moves, but when our "Baby, It's Cold Outside" video got picked up everywhere, the comments section devolved into a gladiator pit of hate, with people using our content as a weapon. It was "You pathetic hippy snowflakes" versus "You deplorable Trumpsters." It was a dumpster fire of meanness, and it was happening on our turf. I wanted to extinguish it immediately.

It was happening so fast that I couldn't moderate the comments by myself, so I got on the phone with Facebook, trying to get the worst of the worst people blocked. (We're talking about people making threats like "I hope someone rapes *you*.") I was trying to keep my voice from wobbling as I described what was going on when Penn came in, bright as a summer day, singing, "We're a hit!"

I got off the phone and said, "Please tell me you're kidding. People are using our video as ammunition in a war I don't want to be in. People are being hurt in *our* comment section."

Penn shrugged and said, "Oh, don't read the comments."

Listen, I know there are people out there who don't read their comments, but that's not how I roll. To me, you're missing out on the beauty of the platform if you don't engage with the people who take the time to watch what you make, and 99.9 percent of the time that engagement brings me joy and a feeling of connection. But in this case, my reaction was *Shut. It. Down. Delete the video. I want out.*

I asked Penn, "Can't we just take it down?" He looked at me as though I had just suggested we have maggots with a side of poison ivy for dinner and said, "Are you nuts? This is huge for us."

My logical mind acknowledged the truth of what he'd just said, but my empath heart just couldn't handle it. Plus I do not like being called crazy.

I curled up into a chair in a dark corner of our bedroom. Penn waltzed in again to say, "Isn't this incredible?" He wanted me to share his joy, but I was rocking back and forth on the verge of sucking my thumb.

He looked at me, genuinely puzzled, and said, "Can't you just be happy?"

I sat straight up in my chair. "Excuse me? '*Just* be happy?'" I said. I live with anxiety and depression. It takes a lot for me to be happy on a good day. Add in some internet trolls and I don't stand a chance. I shouted, "DON'T YOU EVEN KNOW WHO I AM?"

I'M NOT EMOTIONAL; *YOU'RE* EMOTIONAL

Emotions are slippery little suckers, and it doesn't take much pressure for them to slide out of control if they are at the base of your argument. When you disagree about a practical issue like who is doing more housework or whether you should be having more sex, you know that, in an ideal world, there is a way to have that conversation calmly, using logic and rational thought. But when you fight about your emotions, it will nearly always feel volatile, and when things are volatile, sometimes they go *kablooey* and someone gets hurt.

We have certainly been left nursing our wounds after we fight about emotions, but we're going to brag again here. "Baby, It's Cold Outside" short circuit aside, we are usually pretty good at partnering our way through each other's emotions. This is particularly important for us because each of us struggles with an actual mental health issue. As Kim mentioned, she has anxiety and depression, which we will talk more about later in this chapter, and Penn has

ADHD. Through the years, we have figured out how to keep our emotional states from derailing our marriage.

In this chapter, we'd like to help you figure out a healthy way to be emotionally connected to your partner without losing yourself. Get ready, because along the way we are going to completely contradict what you think you want in a relationship, and then we are going to try to persuade you to say what your partner most wants to hear in every argument—"You are right"—*and mean it.*

But before we go any further, we want to remind you yet again that we are not doctors, therapists, psychologists, psychiatrists, or even veterinarians. What we share in this chapter is drawn from our experience as people who struggle but who have figured out how to live well and supportively with someone else who struggles. Both of us have gone to experts, people with actual degrees, to get help with our issues, and we would advise you to do the same if you are grappling with a significant challenge. What we're here to help with is how to make sure your crap is *your* crap and not your partner's crap. (Told you we're not doctors.)

BORDER CONTROL

Take a peek at the statements below. Circle the ones that best describe how you feel about your relationship with your partner.

A

- I am so close to my partner that sometimes it feels like we are living in the same skin.
- When my partner is down in the dumps, I can't be happy.

- I like to check in with my partner before making any decision, big or small.
- My partner knows me so well that they understand everything about me.
- My partner and I agree on nearly everything.

B

- If my partner criticizes me, I might not like it, but I take it in stride.
- It is not always important to please my partner.
- If my partner is upset, it is equally likely that the reason is an issue unrelated to me as it is something I've done.
- I am comfortable with my partner going places and doing things without me.
- If I argue with my partner, I can move on easily.

Those first statements are pretty romantic, aren't they? But if you circled more items from set A than set B, perhaps it's time to take a good look at whether you are making choices that reflect your own values, beliefs, and emotions, or if there is a possibility that you may be custom-tailoring your reactions to situations in the hopes of feeling more connected to your partner. There's no shame in this. We all take other people's emotions into account to some degree. (All of us except sociopaths.)

On the surface, it might not seem like a bad thing to identify with your partner's feelings, but when you let your partner's emotions cloud your own, you obscure your authentic sense of who you are. You become, in the words of psychologist Murray Bowen, "an undifferentiated family ego mass," basically a big blob of emotions.

Gross, right? When you identify too closely with your partner's feelings, it's hard to disentangle your own.

Think of it this way: Imagine you are scuba diving with your partner and they swim after a shiny fish. On the way, they kick up some sand and sediment from the ocean floor, maybe even scare an octopus who squirts its weird inky juice into the water. Before they can get to the fish, their mask is obscured by sea gunk floating around. If you paddle into the murk after them, before too long, you're going to be just as turned around as they are.

If you want to see things clearly, you need to swim near your partner but in your own part of the ocean.

As creatures who relate to one another, humans live in a constant state of push-pull between the desire to be close to other people and the desire to be independent. (Therapists call this the Family Systems Theory, brainchild of the aforementioned Murray Bowen.) It can feel like trying to thread a needle in a hurricane when you're aiming for that sweet spot between having a loving, intimate, empathetic relationship while acting according to your own thoughts, feelings, beliefs, and values.

Anyone who has ever been around someone when their emotions have taken hold of them knows how tricky this is.

PENN

It was definitely hard for me to hold on to my own feelings of joy when Kim couldn't share them. When that video hit, I wanted to hire a skywriter to poot out, "75,000,000 views!" and then hire a second pilot to fly me in loops through all of those zeroes. Kim's balloon *pfffffft* really harshed my mellow, if I can use a 1990s college term.

To tell you the truth, while she was spiraling, I wanted to get out of the house. You know what? I did. I didn't have to go far from home to find responses that were more in line with my own. I walked out into my front yard and, before I even got to the sidewalk, someone drove by and hollered, "That video was so awesome!" *You got that right, buddy.* I decided to celebrate our success in my own way. I played probably five or six sets of tennis that day. (Things get wild when you are in your forties.)

But the whole time, there was this pesky bird from a horror movie following me, crowing, "Yes, but what about Kim? Caw, what about Kim?" It was really hard to enjoy myself to the fullest when the person I care about the most in this world was sinking into a tar pit of despair.

It was like I had caught her sadness.

GOING VIRAL

That is exactly what happened. Have you ever started a conversation in a perfectly good mood only to have the person you're talking to moan and groan about the fender bender they got into on the way to having their fifth root canal? How did you feel after that? Or maybe you were feeling a little blah at work, but your coworker came over jazzed about a new idea, and by the time she left your office, you felt a little more energized about making it to five o'clock. Scientists have studied this phenomenon and confirmed that it's true: our moods are contagious, and, in a shock to no one, bad moods are more contagious than good moods. Researchers analyzed depression screenings in high school students and found that kids whose friends were bummed out were more likely to be in a bad mood themselves. Another study found that simply observing someone through a one-way mirror as they have a stressful experience increased the likelihood that the subject's stress hormone levels would rise. And when the person getting stressed out was someone the subject knew, those levels increased even more. So imagine how susceptible you are to the mood of the person you eat, drink, laugh, live, sleep, and in our case, work with. Your partner's moods are a virulent contagion.

If the words *virulent contagion* conjure up unpleasant images from COVID-19 or an image of someone in one of those hazmat suits people wear in movies when they're handling a monkey virus or whatever is worse than Ebola, that is exactly what we are trying to convey. Mood contagions make it hard to maintain autonomous emotional health.

NOT ONE, AND DEFINITELY NOT THE SAME

A second reason it is hard to maintain clearly defined emotional borders is that we *want* to believe that our partners see things the way we do. It affirms our sense of the world. When we share a point of view with someone, we think, *Yes, that is how things are. I knew it!* Consequently, we frequently make the mistake of assuming our partners will have the same emotional response in a given situation we would. When they don't, we feel an unsettling distance open up between us. A tiny part of us says in a naggy voice, *Hey, if we aren't responding to this in the same way, is this maybe not my person after all? Shouldn't we be more aligned on this? Gulp.* So we recalibrate our reactions to make them similar to theirs. That only distances us from feeling like our authentic selves, which, of course, is how we should actually feel around our partners.

We are here to tell you that it is okay for you to be different from your partner. Not just the kind of different where you like different things—I like a double espresso and you like a pumpkin spice latte, or you are an exercise addict and all my pants smell like the couch—but truly, actually different, with different feelings and values and reactions to events.

None of us have had the same set of experiences, let alone genes, so there are going to be times when you hear "Laurel," and your partner hears "Yanny." You see a blue-and-black dress, and your partner sees a white-and-gold dress. You see half-full; your partner sees half-empty. Humans can't even all agree as a species whether cilantro tastes good or not, so it is unreasonable to think that when it comes to something as complex and multifaceted as our emotions, we'll share the same ones.

Here's the thing: your ideas, impressions, emotions, beliefs, and actions are not any more meaningful if they are shared by your partner. Is that thought a little scary? We get it. It can stop you cold when someone you love surprises you with their emotional reaction.

KIM

Or with their *lack* of an emotional reaction. Let me give you an example of what I mean.

Recently, we had to clear Penn's dad's things out of his condo in order to get him into a new care facility. We had a 6:00 a.m. flight to make the following morning, but at 10:00 p.m., we were still at his dad's unit. We had been there for hours, cleaning stuff out and getting him ready to move.

I kept checking in with Penn as we went through boxes and boxes of keepsakes and mementos, asking "Are you good? Sit and talk to me."

Each time, he replied, "What? Nope, I'm good . . . Should we throw out this dehumidifier?"

And then it was just plunk, plunk, plunk into trash bins. Entire photo albums, gone in an instant. This was a lifetime of memories, most of which were irreplaceable.

I wasn't going to let it go. I was like, "Penn, are you sure you're okay with this?"

He insisted: "I'm fine."

I went back to sorting through tablecloths, and then a few minutes later I noticed him stuffing something into a bag to throw away. It was his father's clerical robe.

I had to say something. His dad had been a Presbyterian minister for forty years, a total rock star in his community, beloved by so many people. He'd worn that robe with its gorgeous handmade collar for decades. I stopped again and asked, "Honey, don't you want to save that?"

He just said, "Kim, if we start saving all this stuff, it's going to take over our house."

I'm incredibly sentimental—I have trouble throwing away a gum wrapper if I have shared the pack with one of my kids—so inside, I was wondering, *How can you be good with this? You are clearly in denial.* I felt like one of us had to be depressed about it. One of us had to feel it.

My inclination was to swoop in and minister to him, but I realized that there was no point in trying to make Penn feel sad or wistful. That just wasn't the tune he was humming. He was simply having a different reaction than I would have if I were in his shoes. I went back to sorting linens, and I tried to let him feel his feelings without making them my feelings. (BTW, there is a beautiful hand-embroidered robe in our attic right now if you're looking for one. Text me.)

YOU DO NOT COMPLETE ME

We dare you to try to think of a line from a movie that epitomizes fairy tale romance more fully than Tom Cruise telling Renée Zellweger, "You complete me" in *Jerry Maguire*. Okay, brace yourself, but we absolutely *loathe* that idea, and we 100 percent reject it. The idea that you must be fully merged with someone else to be complete is just bullshit. (Our publisher told us we could use that word one time in this book, and we think this is so important that we're deploying it now.) It's a lovely thought, but it is total and utter nonsense. The notion that we should complete not just each other's sentences, but each other, is nothing more than a terrible, horrible, no good, very bad myth. If you are looking for a partner who completes you, you are looking for the wrong things in a relationship.

Listen, we are each other's favorite people. We miss each other when we are not together, and when we are old and gray, one of us is going to die and the other will die seven minutes later because we will be so sad. But we each have our own stuff we're working out, and we can't depend on the other to solve it for us.

We hear people say things like "When I find the right person, it's not going to matter that my job is terrible." Or "When I fall in love, I won't be depressed anymore." But guess what? It doesn't work that way. Your crap follows you.

Mister Rogers always said, "There is only one like you in the whole world. There's never been anyone exactly like you before, and there will never be again." That guy didn't just have great sweaters; he was smart. Your partner doesn't complete you; you are already complete.

In a healthy partnership, it's not so much that your partner completes you as it is that they bring out the whole you and let you be your real self. The ideal mate is more like a lamp shining its warm light on you than a puzzle piece snapping into place.

Are you ready for more tough love? It's not your partner's job to solve your problems, and it is not your job to solve theirs. Your job is to walk with your partner, not to come to their rescue. You've got to handle your own business and let them handle theirs.

Let's think about that scuba diving scenario again. When you are in a scuba suit, you are capable of breathing completely on your own. You don't need someone else pulling off your mask and shoving their breathing tube in your face. You have your own totally functional tank.

Coming to terms with this is as hard as it sounds. It is a lifelong project.

PENN

I love every single thing about my wife. Every inch of her face and her body and every personality trait. I love her sense of humor, and I love how she is so in touch with herself and how she keeps me in line, because Lord knows I need that.

But while it's true that I *love* every single thing about my wife, I don't *understand* everything about my wife.

Sometimes, it becomes crystal clear that she is a creature whose interior life I cannot begin to comprehend. If you have a dog, do you ever look at them and wonder, *Is this dog happy, or is this dog absolutely miserable?* Our dog, Sunny, is adorable and energetic and wags her tail all the time. But if we were to drive her into the middle of nowhere and let her run off into the wilderness, would she be happier? We honestly cannot tell. (Note to PETA and animal lovers everywhere: WE WOULD SOONER SPRINKLE BEDBUGS ON

OUR COMFORTER THAN DO THIS.) That's how I feel about Kim sometimes. Her moods are a mystery to me.

I want to be one of those *Star Trek* creatures that can read someone's mind when they touch them, so I can finally know for sure whether Kim is happy. It kills me sometimes not to know what she is thinking or feeling.

But early on in our marriage, I learned that I am not going to understand her at every moment. When we first got engaged, we moved into an apartment in New York. It was a very small space, and we were around each other all the time. Somewhere around the third night of our living together, Kim looked around and was suddenly *furious* about our apartment. Nothing about it was making her happy: not the rug, not the unfathomably expensive curtains—Why are these so expensive? They're just rectangles of fabric!—not the fact that it had a ceiling.

I went into fix-it mode. I washed the dishes. I moved our pile of shoes into the closet. I even tried to move the couch to a different spot so we could have more space. She took one look and said, "This place looks like crap," and then she started crying. My immediate reaction was, "Oh my, you're really unhappy. Should we not have gotten engaged? I'll move the couch back!"

KIM

I didn't need Penn to move that couch. I needed him to recognize that I was sad. There were a million stressors in my life at that time—new job, new town, new fiancé, first time away from my family—plus that couch was totally better by the window where it was before. But as much as I love Penn, he cannot fix what's going on in my brain. Expecting him to do so is a recipe for disaster.

I've battled depression and anxiety my entire adult life. For me, happiness is a muscle. I have to work on it. My default setting rests somewhere between mildly overwhelmed and sheer panic. I've learned I have to do the annoying but necessary things like sleep well, eat right, and reduce my alcohol intake. I have to exercise, meditate, journal. It takes a lot of work for me to exist on this planet as a functioning adult. When the sun is shining and I've done my work, I am by all standards a happy person. When I skimp on sleep, skip the gym, or have too many glasses of wine, my world seems darker.

I will give myself a little credit: I'm very self-aware about when I'm under the cloud. I can say, "This is what I'm feeling, and this is what I need."

Trying to move the couch and his reaction after "Baby, It's Cold Outside" were times when Penn didn't handle my emotions well. But most of the time he's very good at partnering with my depression and anxiety. He's figured out when to back off and then when to walk beside me. He doesn't try to solve my problem, but he will ask, "What do you need right now? Do you need to be in bed under the covers? Do you need me to tell you to get out of bed? Do you need me to take charge, or do you need me to give you space?"

Sometimes I'll say, "I need you to go away." And he's like, "Okay, got it." Or sometimes I'll say, "I need you to tell me to go for a walk."

For me, personally, exercise always helps. We work from home, so getting out of the house makes a world of difference. I have what I call a twelve-minute rule for myself. I have to be active for twelve minutes. If I get on the treadmill or go for a walk or a run, I do it for a minimum of twelve minutes. If after twelve minutes I still feel like crap, I can quit. Yet 100 percent of the time I keep going. It helps me to take control of my mood, but I know the only person who can put one foot in front of the other on hard days is me.

TRUST, THEN VALIDATE

While you are the only person in the world who can handle your business, that's not to say that you should set your partner loose with a "Welp, I'm going to focus on me. Looks like you're on your own, honey."

There can be such loneliness and a feeling of helplessness when your emotions take over. Think of the words we use to describe how it feels when we are emotional. We say we are *overwhelmed, overpowered, overtaken, consumed, possessed, transported, swallowed.* All of those are pretty big. The last thing you need when you are in the grip of a powerful emotion is an added layer of anxiety about whether your feelings are normal. That's why we want you to validate your partner's feelings. You don't have to pretend to share those feelings; you merely need to acknowledge that theirs fall on the spectrum of natural human emotion.

One last time with the scuba diving metaphor: when your partner is in turbid water, you don't need to rescue your partner from the murk, but you do have to let them know that you didn't hightail it for the boat. They need to know that you're going to be there when the sand settles and the ink disperses. When you give credence to your partner's feelings, you are letting them know you are right there in the water with them.

Remember, we're looking for that sweet spot between closeness and independence. The best way to hold on to your emotions and help your partner with theirs is to acknowledge and validate your partner's feelings, no matter how different they are from your own.

KIM

When Penn asked me why I couldn't just be happy about the video, it was very much like he had left me at the bottom of the sea.

I felt the familiar signs of anxiety starting to prickle underneath my skin. Before long, it felt like someone was standing on my chest. My breath got short. I couldn't eat. I couldn't sleep. I needed my partner to understand me, not be one more person who says, "You're crazy!"

When I spiraled out over the video, I needed Penn to get on the floor with me, hold my hand, and offer something along the lines of, "I hear you. I get what you're saying. I know this is how you're wired. I'm here."

I needed him to understand that my mood and my feelings on this were valid, and I had a right to these feelings.

TELL YOUR PARTNER EXACTLY WHAT THEY WANT TO HEAR

If you're the type to read relationship books, and clearly you are, you've probably encountered the expression, "You can be right, or you can be married," meaning that insisting on being right when you fight is deadly in a relationship. When people say this, it's because in most battles, there is ground to be won. I want you to do the dishes; you want me to be more affectionate. Either someone breaks out a sponge or pulls you in for a cuddle or not. However, when you're talking about emotions, there is no right or wrong. You can be right *and* married. So try these magic words: when you and your partner are having different emotional reactions in a tense situation, turn the heat down by saying, "*You're right.* It *does* feel X when Y happens," knowing fully well that *you are also right* because all feelings are equally valid. You don't even need to cross your fingers behind your back.

Let us tell you a story about a woman we worked with once

named Becky. A few years ago, she and her husband, Peter, and their two kids were settling in to their first house. Before the new-house smell had faded, Becky went down to the basement to do some laundry. Just as she was loading the dryer, out of the corner of her eye she detected a distinct wiggling motion. *What the . . . ?* She turned around in time to see a snake (!) slither into a tiny hole in the foundation. She shrugged and went back to loading the laundry.

NOT!

She dropped her wet towels on the floor, sprinted upstairs, and immediately pulled Peter into the kitchen to whisper as calmly as she could that there was an *ake-snay* in the *asement-bay.*

He just laughed.

She repeated herself. Clearly, he had not understood, so this time she added, "What if it's poisonous?"

Peter responded, "That is nuts. There is a 0 percent chance it is poisonous. Plus, I think you mean venomous. Poisonous means . . ."

He didn't have a chance to finish his biology lesson. She disappeared into their room to look for a reptile-free home on Zillow.

Okay, yeah, chances were that it was not someone's pet cottonmouth that had escaped, but were the chances really *zero*? Was she totally bonkers to worry? To be clear, she absolutely did not want Peter to flip out—someone had to finish doing the laundry after all. She just wanted her experience and feelings acknowledged and validated.

Happily, after a while, Peter came upstairs, sat down beside her, and said, "You're right. That *would* be scary if that snake were poisonous. But I still think you meant venomous." Let's give Peter a B-minus. (Points for eventually validating Becky's feelings, but he needs to work on the mansplaining.)

PENN

As good as Kim is at handling her feelings, she is equally good at acknowledging mine. I have these microperiods (I know I just made this term up, and I have no firsthand perspective of what women's menstruation feels like, but these are my feelings so please validate them. See: Book, The Rest of.) when I get down in the dumps, and nearly every time I'm like, *WTF is going on?* The source can be hard to pinpoint, which makes the feeling even worse. It's not like wintertime triggers bad feelings or having too many beers pushes me over the edge. I just get bummed out. It's as if whatever chemical in my brain makes me think the glass is half-full takes a break for a couple of days. All of a sudden, the glass is half-empty. This is so embarrassing, but one time, I even googled to see if there was such a thing as a male period. (And there is, kind of—we get a drop in testosterone sometimes that affects our mojo. Look it up.)

On a deeper level, I have had anxiety attacks. They are awful. I've never had a near-death experience, but I feel like I have. When I am in the throes of an attack, my heart pounds against my rib cage like it's trying to escape, my palms get sweaty, the blood in my neck and face heats up to eight thousand degrees, and my head swims like someone piped in toxic gas. It's impossible to predict when one is going to hit. I pray you never have one.

When I have an attack, Kim is an expert at letting me know that I'm not alone and that I'm not a freak—or on the brink of death. She'll sit down with me and ask if I'm having this or that symptom. Then she'll nod reassuringly and say, "That's completely normal. You're not having a heart attack; you're having a panic attack. Those feelings are wretched, but what you're experiencing is totally natural."

She doesn't say it like, "You're a wuss. Buck up, dummy." She says it like, "Yeah, this sucks. Just so you know, you're very healthy. This happens to so many people. I'll be here while you ride it out." It makes me feel 1,000 percent better to know that it's not all in my head and that I have a partner who will love me through it.

How to Validate Your Partner's Feelings

At first, it might not feel natural to validate your partner's feelings because humans are so conditioned to try to win when we fight. But with practice you'll get better at acknowledging what your partner is experiencing—and they'll feel better (and closer to you) when you do. Try to use language that acknowledges whatever feeling they are having. Here are a few examples:

Scenario: Your partner's boss slighted them in a meeting full of coworkers.
Instead of: "What are you so worked up about? That wasn't personal. She's hard on everyone."
Use magic words: "Man, I'm really sorry. That sucks."

Scenario: You've had a near miss at a busy intersection.
Instead of: "Calm down. Everything is fine."
Use magic words: "I see why you are upset. That was close. I'm glad we're okay."

Scenario: Your partner has a couple too many at a party and is worried about their behavior.
Instead of: "No one even noticed."

Use magic words: "I'm not judging you, but man, it would be painful if someone talked behind your back. I know how important it is to you that people respect you."

Scenario: Someone cut in line in front of your partner at the grocery store.
Instead of: "Let's keep things in perspective. What's the big whoop?"
Use magic words: "No wonder you're angry. That's not fair."

Scenario: You're behind on your credit card payment.
Instead of: "It's no big deal. You can pay the minimum."
Use magic words: "You're right. Why is money so hard? Falling behind is so stressful."

Scenario: You're sending your child to sleepaway camp for the first time.
Instead of: "Relax. Nothing is going to happen."
Use magic words: "It would be terrible if something happened. I can understand why you're stressed."

To recap, the healthiest relationship is one where you are connected to your partner but still totally yourself. This is hard because emotions are contagious and because we foolishly want to believe that our partners see everything the way we do. Trying to separate your partner's emotions from your own can be as frustrating as untangling a snarled necklace, but it is worth it. So go ahead: handle your own business, validate your partner's feelings, and then brag to all your friends about it.

03

CAN YOU PLEASE JUST SAY SOMETHING? ANYTHING? ANYTHING AT ALL?

THE FIGHT

KIM

We are suckers for our dogs. Maybe you've noticed on social media that we treat our dog like the world revolves around her. Maybe you've noticed we've named her *Sunny*. Like, um, how the earth revolves around the sun. That pup is sunshine on four legs. I could spend all day taking photos and videos of her and then staring at them on my phone even when she is still in the room. But Sunny is not the first dog we fell in love with. Before Sunny, there was Ruby. Oh, Ruby. My heart still does one of those roller-coaster drops just typing her name.

We adopted Ruby when she was about four or five months old. We brought her home on a Friday and had a dog trainer at our home on Sunday. We joined puppy classes, did in-home drills, and even sent her to live with a trainer for three weeks. At eight months old, she passed her Canine Good Citizen test. We had visions of our pup becoming a therapy dog, helping people in schools and hospitals. Ruby was a perfect student, but she was an even better companion. I'd feed her in the morning, and we'd snuggle for a few minutes while my coffee brewed. She'd rest her head on my lap while I checked emails, and then I'd say, "Go wake up the kids," and she'd run upstairs and lick their faces. Back then, we had just gone through a period of wondering if we should have a third child, but once we got Ruby we agreed that there was no need. Ruby made our family complete.

But one afternoon when Ruby was around nine months old, we left our front door unlocked for a photographer who was setting up for a video shoot. We heard the door shut and then after a few minutes, we heard a commotion and dashed downstairs to see what had happened. Our photographer was sitting on the floor, looking stunned. "Your dog bit me when I walked in," he said. She didn't break the skin, and he was gracious about it, but we were rattled. What was that about?

We thought it was a one-time thing, but a few weeks later, we had a new babysitter watch the kids. Ruby had started jumping on guests as they entered, so when the doorbell rang, we held her down by the collar as the sitter walked in. Little did we know that for dogs with protective instincts, this is the *worst* way to try to restrain them. It's like you're winding them up so they can spring for an attack. So when we let go of her collar, Ruby jumped up and bit the new sitter. This time, she broke the skin. Watching it happen was like watching a baby swing a machete. It just didn't make any sense. How could our sweet, obedient dog have hurt someone?

After Ruby bit the babysitter, we hired a dog behaviorist and then another. But the bites kept coming. She bit Penn's dad, Lola's friend's mom, and a stranger when I took her for a run. Finally, the last trainer we hired said what we knew but had refused to hear: "You have a dog that bites people. You have children. You're playing with fire if you don't find her a new home." I cut that trainer a check and showed her the door.

When I thought about giving up Ruby, I couldn't sleep. At night, I crawled to the floor and lay with her as long as she would let me. What kind of trainer suggests getting rid of your own dog? I mean, did people actually do that sort of thing? Forget it. I put the idea out of my head.

Then it happened again. This time, Ruby bit my twenty-two-year-old niece. She had just moved nearby and she'd done a great job getting to know Ruby. She could walk into the house without Ruby even paying attention. But one night all the lights were off downstairs, and our niece had to drop by the house to return a casserole dish she'd borrowed. I was upstairs putting away Christmas decorations when I heard the "Ow!" My blood froze. Our niece had unlocked the door with her key and walked in like she had a hundred times before. Ruby must not have been able to tell it was her because it was dark (can you tell I'm still trying to rationalize this?), and she bit her—hard.

PENN

I'm gonna jump in here.

On the day that Kim told me that Ruby had bitten a stranger during a run, she was trembling—not because she was scared of our dog or scared of getting sued. She was scared that there was no way to avoid it any longer: Ruby needed to go. But instead of accepting the obvious and putting it into words, my wife turned into a fire wall of anger and defiance, shouting that we needed more training, more restrictions, and a new approach to managing our dog.

I knew the right thing to do was to talk it through calmly and help Kim understand what had been clear to me since the first bite—Ruby needed a new home. I wanted to say, "Honey, this is the end. It is time to make an impossibly awful decision." But I couldn't do it. Instead, I shook my head and walked away, and here's why: we'd gotten Ruby during a period of our lives when Kim's anxiety and depression were the worst I'd ever seen. I'd say that she was in a funk, but that sounds too cute for the "life is despair, there's no way out, and I can't think of a reason to get out of bed in the morning" vibes she was radiating like a nuclear reactor right before meltdown. I hated seeing her like that, so when I saw a spark flicker in her eyes when she suggested that we volunteer to help a dog rescue organization transport puppies the last mile home, I said, "Sign me up."

I'm not a moron. I knew there was more to Kim's agenda for that outing than logging some volunteer hours, but it was eating my soul to see my wife that sad. So we got in the car and drove to meet a Winnebago that had just driven twenty dogs for twenty hours from a kill shelter in Louisiana to find them homes in North Carolina. Kim and I loaded a bunch of cute little black dogs and a handful of butter-colored pups into cars so they could reach their forever homes. Then one of the other volunteers put one last dog into Kim's arms, and my wife's body immediately curled protectively around that ball of fur like it was a baby—and then she started talking to it like it was a baby. "Oh, da puppy. Look at dis puppy," she cooed. A blind man could see that dog was now ours.

We had nothing at home—no crate, no dog food, no newspaper. We didn't even have a fenced yard. But Kim looked happier than I'd seen her in months, so when she said, "You do realize we're taking her home, right?"

I nodded. "All right." Welcome to the family, Ruby.

Kim lit up. "Yay! You get to go home with us," she said into a belly of puppy fur. That day, we brought home a canine Prozac pill for my wife—one that turned out to have really bad side effects.

Ruby came to us with fleas, worms, and bite marks on her ears. We cleaned her up, bought a pet store's worth of supplies, and then obsessed over her every move. We all loved having her around, but Kim loved her the hardest. The way my wife's mood changed seemed like a small miracle.

And then the biting started.

I knew it was over the very first time she put her little doggy teeth onto a human body. I have a lot of good qualities, but being supernaturally observant is not one of them. It's not like I'm some sort of doggy Jedi. *Anyone* could see that Ruby was not having normal dog reactions to being around other people, and it made our whole family anxious. Ruby freaked out anytime someone came over to our house. Every time the doorbell rang, we all held our breaths. We crated her, locked her behind the powder room door, or sent her to our bedroom. It was like we were harboring a dangerous criminal, and we were always one *woof* away from the authorities raiding our home.

Our house started to feel like a prison—and then Kim took away visitation rights. She said, "We're just going to have to be one of those families that doesn't have people in our house." You guys, we live *in the South*. For those of you who haven't had the honor, let me tell you something about southern neighbors: a closed door is indistinguishable from a welcome mat. People in the South are forever swinging open the screen door unannounced carrying a pasta salad and hollering, "Y'all home?" When Kim said, "We just have to be one of those families that doesn't have people over," what I should have said right there was, "This dog is not working for this family."

But I didn't. I deflected, sometimes with humor, sometimes with chores, sometimes by hiring another person to give us another opinion on how to control our dog. Neither of us managed to say what needed to be said until we had completely wrecked our lives for almost a year.

How could we have fixed this sooner?

YOU GOTTA FIGHT FOR YOUR RIGHT TO STAY MARRIED

Did you notice anything about this fight? There was *no fight.* And that, friends, was precisely the problem. We *needed* to fight.

Yep. You read that right. We are actually advocating fighting with your spouse—as long as you do it right. When something is bothering you, you might think it's better to endure in silence, to play the part of the stoic or the martyr. Choosing that path may even sound like you're being the bigger person, taking the good ol' high road. *Au contraire.* When you say, "I'm above that" or "I'm not going to respond to that" or "I'm not going to dignify that with a response," you are compromising your communication. Those are all phrases that emphasize separation, and, worse, they are a power play. When you refuse to acknowledge a difficult issue, you are signaling to your partner, "I set the agenda in this house."

Christopher tells us that refusing to engage with your partner, or *stonewalling*, is a way of asserting power and control. When you stonewall, you refuse to talk about a problem because it is difficult or inconvenient, building a wall behind which the problem only grows. But we're here to tell you that is the path of the coward. If you want to have a relationship that goes somewhere, you can't avoid every difficult stretch of road. You have to drive over those potholes, go over those speed bumps, get stuck in the mud. Let your communication idle too long, and you're going to run out of fuel.

Listen, we know that fighting with your spouse is as much fun as doing your taxes. But like doing your taxes, it is far better to get your butt in a chair—otherwise you are going to end up paying a serious penalty. Of course, this is a lesson we've learned by failing.

In this chapter, with Christopher's help, we are going to talk about why you stonewall, examine why it's so damaging to your relationship, and then give you a sledgehammer to knock down that wall.

WHY WE STONEWALL

In every relationship, there are things that are hard to talk about—not just in the moment, but always. Maybe it's that extra beer your partner has after dinner, or the way she laughs really hard at another man's joke, or the fact that another year went by without a promotion—and both people avoid talking about the issue as if ignoring it will starve it of the oxygen it needs to survive. It is terribly tempting to avoid talking about something. It always seems easier than engaging. Ask any kid during report card season.

But let's look at how not talking about a problem creates distance between you and your partner and why we allow that to happen.

Have you ever had any of the following thoughts?

- This will probably blow over.
- I don't want to make a fuss.
- It's their business, not mine.
- What if I'm blowing it out of proportion?
- They're an adult. They can handle it.
- If they don't want to talk about it, I won't bring it up. I don't want to nag.

You know what we say to that kind of self-talk? *Bawkbawk-bawkbawk*. Okay, that was harsh, but it comes from a loving place. While we justify our lack of action with benevolent-sounding excuses, the truth is, we don't broach difficult topics for one of two reasons: (1) because they make us uncomfortable, and we are huge wimps who try to minimize discomfort whenever possible, and (2) because sometimes we grow perversely attached to our grievances.

Are we saying that we actually hold on to our silence when it is, as was the case with Ruby, obviously destructive? Yes. Because silence can be protective. Christopher has told us that we stonewall when we feel fear and want to protect ourselves. As a frontline defense against getting hurt further, we fashion a blockade out of our anger and resentment. We lay a stone made of "I am so afraid of how you will react!" on top of a stone made of "I am so angry that you cannot see how much this is affecting me," on top of a stone made of "I resent you for hurting me." Pretty soon, you have an unbreachable barrier preventing you from connecting with your partner on the other side.

When you surround yourself with stone walls, you can make a nice little airtight fortress for yourself, free of any discordant ideas. It's safe in there, and, just as important, life is predictable. You're in control. You can spend your days staring at those stones, focusing on their steady shape to your heart's content without ever concerning yourself about what is on the other side and how it might change your view. But the moment you shove aside one of those stones to take a peek, your fortress is breached, and a new view could come through that window. That light has the annoying habit of highlighting what you've kept hidden in the darkness, so often you slide the stone back, encasing yourself once more.

PENN

While Ruby was living with us, I was absolutely protecting myself by stonewalling. When I put up a wall between me and Kim on the subject of Ruby, it was partially because I was worried that Kim was going to lash out and call me heartless if I suggested that we find Ruby a new home. After all, as far as Kim was concerned, Ruby was our child. What kind of person abandons a family member? Had I no loyalty?

I justified holding my tongue by telling myself that the minute I said aloud that Ruby needed to go, Kim would realize I was right, which usually I would love. But in this case, I was worried she would crash because her puppy Prozac was going to be taken away. I thought she was going to feel like she had failed and she might spiral into an even deeper, darker place than she was in before she got the dog. Talking about our dog problem seemed like a total no-win situation. Kim would be devastated. The kids would be devastated. Kim would be angry at me. She would be angry at herself. I would be the bad guy.

So I retreated behind my wall.

KIM

Credit where credit is due: Penn was right. I couldn't fathom giving up on that dog, but not talking about the problem created an impossible, unsustainable tension in our lives and our marriage. I wanted no part of a conversation that ended with us giving up on Ruby. We had made a commitment to this animal, and I didn't want to hear anything else, so I refused to talk about the possibility.

I could teach a master class on avoiding conflict. Pre-Penn, I had relationships in which my boyfriend and I could operate in silence for *days* at a time. We'd go without talking for so long that I'd forget how the fight even started. (There's a reason I'm not married to any of those guys.)

Not talking about things was my *jam*, and I'd learned that song young. My parents really were great humans, but they should not have been married to each other. They stayed together for the kids even though they were clearly mismatched, and as a result, they did not talk about *anything*. Our family dinners were weirdly silent. My parents had polite exchanges along the lines of "Who is going to pick the kids up tomorrow?" or "This is a lovely dinner, thank you," but what was left unsaid, always, was, "Oh, yeah, and we are not fundamentally compatible. Should we maybe do something about that?" I spent my formative years watching them erect the Great Stone Wall of China.

THE SOUND OF SILENCE

If it's so hard to bring up a tough topic, why bother to do it at all? The answer is that the alternative is worse. We hate to be the bearers of bad news, but no less of a luminary than number one relationship guru smart guy John Gottman identified stonewalling as one of the signs of relationship apocalypse. *Shudder.* Refusing to engage sends the sign that you simply do not care, and when we feel like our partners do not care, it freaks us out—our words, not Gottman's.

Refusing to engage with your partner is serious stuff, so serious that some therapists consider prolonged silent treatment a form of abuse. That's a strong statement—and the cold shoulder would have to turn into a glacier-sized appendage before you could label it abuse—but the fact that it's even a possibility speaks volumes.

The kind of silence we're talking about here is not abusive but it is insidious—and very painful. Purdue University professor of psychology Kipling Williams found that the area of your brain that registers physical pain (the dorsal anterior cingulate cortex, for those of you keeping score at home) also activates when you feel excluded or ignored. He determined that even two or three minutes of being ostracized *by a stranger* can have lasting negative effects on our moods.

Being shut out by our partners is a major stress on our systems—and stress can manifest itself in the body in a ton of really unpleasant ways, causing rashes, diarrhea, high blood pressure, low sex drive, muscle pain, and about a hundred other terrible symptoms.

PENN

Like hair loss. Apparently, stress can make your hair follicles go into a "resting phase"? Mine went into all-out hibernation. When Ruby started biting and we refused to talk about it, I noticed a few stray hairs here and there—and then a few months later *full clumps* came off my skull. Our sink got stopped up, and I was like, "What's that about? Let me check it out." I ran the snake down there, and whoa Nelly, there was an animal pelt in my drain.

It was really stressful living with a dog who bit people, but it was more stressful not talking about it. Every conversation felt like a minefield where we were stepping gingerly around topics that might explode. You'd be surprised how many things remind you of your dog. We avoided neighbors who had dogs of their own, we held our breaths at restaurants hoping the waitress wouldn't offer us a doggy bag, and each morning we woke up thinking, *Okay, it's going to be a good day if our dog doesn't bite someone.* That is a *terrible* metric for what makes a good day. We were constantly aware and constantly vigilant. It made us stressed, it made Ruby stressed, and it made the people around us stressed. The question of "What do you do with a problem like Ruby?" lurked behind everything that we did, but it never fully emerged.

It got heavier and heavier and heavier. My drain got hairier and hairier.

KIM

Penn lost his hair; I lost my mobility. When I feel anxiety, it's like a boot pressing on my chest. When I feel stress, my back seizes up. As Ruby's behavior got worse, I constantly told myself, *It's fine, we're fine, and everything is fine. It's fine. We're fine, we're fine, and we're fine. Everything is fine.* But then my body replied, *Oh, no you're not.* My lower back would freeze as though somebody were tightening a corset around my midsection. I couldn't turn around. I walked with straight legs like a penguin.

Our bodies were saying what our mouths could not.

NAME IT TO TAME IT

We can't overstate the importance of this enough: when silence starts to get loud, you have to name the issue to prevent total system failure. Say it out loud.

You can start by saying how the issue is making you feel. Remember, using the magic words *I feel* is a safe way to proceed in a conversation. Not only does that phrase make the other person more inclined to listen, but it turns out saying how you're feeling actually helps get that feeling under control.

Scientists have studied this phenomenon, proving that naming a negative emotion zaps some of its strength. Psychiatrist and proponent of mindfulness Dan Siegel explains naming your emotions as the "upstairs" brain (where you do your rational thinking and planning) dousing your "downstairs" brain (where those primal fight, flight, or freeze feelings reside) with feel-good chemicals that dampen the fight, flight, or freeze response. Simply saying how you feel out loud helps to take some of the stress away.

Researchers at UCLA did an interesting study using spiders that showed how effective naming your feelings can be at helping you to get them under control. Dr. Michelle Craske asked participants to get up close and personal with a tarantula—even going so far as to touch it if they could. (Shout-out to participants for taking one for the team—there is no way we would sign up for this study.) Then Dr. Craske broke subjects into four groups. She asked the first group to say how they felt about being near the tarantula—e.g., "I'm terrified of that bloody arachnid!" The second group was asked to do some self-talk diminishing their experience—e.g., "Oh, it's not so scary. I could crush it with my boot." The third group was asked to say something that had nothing to do with the spider—e.g., "Doritos are better than Cheetos." The fourth group didn't say anything at all. Dr. Craske let the study participants go about their lives for a week before calling them back for another round of "How close can you get to a big, scary spider?" The participants in the first group not only got closer to the little fellow but they also got less stressed out about it. Putting their fear into words had diminished its impact. How about that?

Another UCLA researcher, Matthew Lieberman, found that

people had a less powerful reaction to a photograph of an angry face if they simply labeled it "angry." (This is a study we can get behind.)

The upshot is that capturing whatever your problem is in words makes it seem more manageable. A label makes the feeling containable. We gave it a try and noticed that we felt a little better after we used *I feel* to start a hard conversation. Not completely, of course, but at least able to wrest ourselves from a swamp of emotions. We could move around more freely, breathe a little easier once the problem was out in the open. Naming the feeling became our first step in being able to talk about our problems. Step two, of course, is to lift up the rug you've been sweeping your problem under and identify what the pile of muck is made of. The trick here is to be specific.

Sometimes, even when we finally work up the courage to get the problem out in the open, we obscure it. We say things like, "That thing you're upset with me about" or "our issue," as if we can make a problem less powerful by making it less specific. We fear that naming an issue will conjure it as if by magic. But when everyone's aware of a problem but nobody is talking about it, the problem is actually far more intimidating—like no matter how scary the monster in a horror movie is, it's never as scary as the anticipation before you see it. Putting your problem into very specific words is like putting a verbal leash on the beast. It may snarl, but at least you know where it is and you don't have to worry about an ambush all day, every day.

Get Concrete

If you are going to get to the bottom of your issue, it's not enough to say, "We have a problem." That amorphous description leaves too much room for guesswork and potential misunderstandings. *You* know that when you say, "We have a problem," you mean how concerned you are about the amount of junk food your partner has been eating, but without more context, your partner might very well think you are referring to the clogged gutters. Before you bring up a problem with your partner, ask yourself, *Would a stranger understand what I'm talking about?* You need to be specific about what the problem is and identify it as concretely as possible, so you can begin to align your ideas of what to do next.

Default: "that issue"
Better: "my issue with your mom"
Magic words: "I feel unappreciated when your mother doesn't say thank you after we've hosted her for dinner."

Default: "your hard time"
Better: "your sadness about losing your grandfather"
Magic words: "I feel powerless when I see how much you are struggling with your grandfather's death."

PENN

Kim is the one who tamed our beast. She finally said Ruby needed to go. After our niece got bitten, Kim came into the bedroom with this crazy sad look where her eyes were twice as big as normal—and she's already got really big eyes. She said, "Ruby just bit Bianca." *Pause, sob, breath, sob.* "I'm exhausted and stressed. We can't do this anymore."

This is going to sound terrible, but I was relieved. I was relieved that the dog bit my niece; that's how big of a problem Ruby had become. It just felt so good to have the problem named instead of living with a haze of stress poisoning the very air we breathed. Our stone walls had been suffocating us.

KIM

At first, I just sobbed. I cried so hard that I popped a blood vessel in my eye. Of course, Ruby came into the room and saw that I was sad and licked my tears, which demolished me.

As much as I hate to admit it, the situation got better after I had finally named the problem out loud. We sent an email to the rescue agency explaining the situation, and they wrote back immediately with a very compassionate message, promising to help find another home for Ruby. The logistics of our life got a lot simpler when we didn't have to worry about protecting everybody. I felt guilty that we could have our neighbors over only because we had rehomed Ruby, but the atmosphere in the house changed. It was like we had opened the windows and we could breathe again.

All the physical symptoms got better too: the pressure in my chest lifted, the tightness in my back unclenched. Penn stopped losing his hair. There was pain and sadness, but there was also some pride mixed in at the courage it had taken to make the hard call.

PENN

This chapter is super sad. I am sorry about that. I've cried twice already. So I'm going to do what I do best: deflect with some humor.

I am writing this outside on my back porch, and Sunny just came out to check on me. I gave her a snuggle and then took a picture of her to send to our neighbor (one of Kim's best friends), who had just texted that she misses seeing Sunny during COVID-19. I sent a shot of Sunny with her head on my lap with the caption "Someone wants a playdate . . ." and copied Kim. Kim wrote me back: "I'm dying." I thought, *Man, Kim is as sad as I am about writing this chapter.*

Wrong. Actually, she was dying from laughter because the lap photo was 10 percent dog, 90 percent crotch. I had just sent a picture of my crotch to Kim's best friend saying, "Someone wants a playdate."

Okay, moving on.

SIT IN THE SUCK

We don't want to act like you are going to want to play "Name that problem" for family game night once you've tried it. Identifying a problem out loud is not a game. It's not fun. In fact, it can be really, really unpleasant. You're not just shattering the silence when you finally speak; you're shattering all those parts of yourself that allowed you to stay silent—the protective resentment, guilt, and accommodation. However, like many things that are good for you—exercise, going to the dentist, eating quinoa—you have to get through the unpleasant part in order to reap the rewards.

Before you can address the problem, you need to sit in the suck.

KIM

My initial instinct when I get into an argument is always to yell "Fine!" slam the door, and then leave. As soon as I so much as catch a glimpse of the suck, I want to head for the hills. I've always been this way.

I'll never forget what happened after my first big fight with Penn. The details of what set us off are lost to time, but I can recall the aftermath like it was yesterday. After we had at it, I got up and walked outside, slamming the door behind me. He followed me outside. What was this man doing? Couldn't he see I was trying to get the heck out of there?

"Where are you going?" he asked.

"I'm going to drive in circles and clear my head," I explained like I was talking to a child.

"But why?" he asked. "We're still going to have to talk about this."

Wait. What had he just said? He wanted to keep talking? You can do that? You can finish a fight?

So began my first healthy relationship.

That was a major record-scratch moment for me. I had always thought, *This is how I am. When things get tough, I bolt. I can't change it. Take it or leave it.*

But Christopher has taught me that when you can sit in the discomfort and assess, *Why is this uncomfortable for me? Why am I trying to get out of here so fast?*—if you can stop your mind from searching for an escape route and sit still for a moment—that's where the conversation happens, that's where change happens, and that's where growth happens.

Now it's rare for me to leave when Penn and I fight. Our compromise is if I really need it, I get five minutes. I'll walk around the driveway, not head for the highway. For the big ones, I need the night before I can have a reasonable conversation about our needs, but eventually, we're calm, we're together, and we're handling things in a productive way. Allowing myself to sit in the suck is not my default setting, but it's working.

EVEN FAST FOOD TAKES TIME

Christopher has a lesson he likes to use with couples he's counseling. He asks them, "How long does it take to get a hamburger at McDonald's?" People answer "two minutes" or "five minutes," and he tells them, "That's how long it takes for them to put it in a bag, but that burger was years in the making. The cow the beef came from had to be raised, the pickles had to be pickled, the wheat for the bun had to be grown, the tomatoes had to be turned into ketchup." His point is that even things we've been accustomed to think of as instantaneous actually take quite a while. It's the same with talking about a problem that you've long ignored. You can't expect to solve it in one quick conversation. Real issues have evolved over time, and it will take time to resolve them. So our final piece of advice in this chapter is to go easy on yourselves. Don't expect to fix the problem you've been ignoring in one all-out sprint of a conversation. Knowing in advance that you will likely need to have a series of conversations lifts the pressure to nail it on the first attempt. You just need to start one.

Start, Don't Finish

Hemingway once said that he had learned "never to empty the well of my writing; but always to stop when there was still something there in the deep part of the well, and let it refill at night from the springs that fed it." The man might not have won any awards in the marriage department (four wives, cheated on them all), but this is sound advice when it comes to talking through an issue. If you are having trouble finding the nerve to knock down a stone wall between you and your partner, start by having the beginning of the conversation, just laying out the bare bones of how you feel and what the problem is—and then stop. Tell your partner that you need to talk to them for five minutes. That's it. No need to come to a resolution in that first conversation; just draw a line around the problem so you both understand the shape of the thing. Then schedule another time to come back to talk about it more once your well is full again.

04

I DO EVERYTHING AND YOU DO NOTHING

THE FIGHT

KIM

Sometimes, being internet famous sucks. For example, I live in constant fear that someone will witness me Hulking out on my kids when I'm shopping and then there will be a bunch of comments on our next video saying things like, "Oh sure, she looks nice and all, but guess what I saw her do in Target?!"

But with great power comes . . . great power. There was one time in particular when I weighed the pros and cons of using our internet platform for my own devices. I almost decided against it, and then

I figured, *Screw it. I'm using this. I am going to harness the power of the internet to bring great shame on my husband and get him to do my bidding. Muhahaha.*

It started in the bathroom. Back in the day, I read all the books on potty training. I know how things are supposed to go down in there. I know how to reward with ~~raisins~~ M&M's and throw a potty parade to celebrate saying farewell to diapers. But you know what lesson those books left out? How to teach your family to replace the mother-loving toilet paper. In the nearly fifteen years I've been married, and twelve years I've been a parent, I am the only one who has ever placed a roll on the metal rod in the bathroom.

This is par for the course at Casa del Holderness. We are a fairly modern family, but somehow, I do most of the work around the house. I shop for and prepare breakfast, lunch, and dinner. I make doctor appointments, rake the lawn, and wash and fold enough laundry to clothe a small-to-medium–sized city. Everything in life is produced for the people in this house, and making sure it runs smoothly requires a lot of forethought on my part.

The week that pushed me to the brink had been taxing. I'd gone head-to-head with every member of the family about leaving wet towels on the floor. I know it might not sound like that big a deal, but a wet towel on the floor destroys me. It's the mildew (or toxic black mold in training, as I like to think of it). I can smell it, I can see it, and I swear I can hear it plotting to infect my family's lungs. That week, there were mountains of wet towels everywhere—in the bathroom, on the laundry room floor, on my bed. I even found one on the dining room table. I don't know how my family did it, but if they were trying to drive me insane, well done.

So this one morning, after being worn down by days of wet towel showdowns, I went into our downstairs bathroom and saw that somebody had used the final square of toilet paper. The cardboard tube was still on the holder. Suddenly, I zoomed out and saw everything clearly. I lived in a house with slobs. I knocked myself out to take care of them night and day, and in that moment, it felt like they couldn't care less about all the effort I put in. I work really, really hard. I do a lot of plate spinning every day, and if one thing crashes down, *boom*, a bunch of other stuff comes crashing down with it.

I started making a list in my head of things that are harder than putting TP on the holder. It had only one item on it: everything. *Everything* is harder. Replacing a toilet paper roll is the easiest thing in the entire world. It was like a shaman had opened my mind to show me the truth of the toilet paper roll. The empty roll wasn't just an affliction of forgetfulness or laziness. No. The failure to change it was a big, fat "I don't respect you. I don't value anything you do for me. But I expect you to keep doing it anyway" written in Charmin. It was a message courtesy of my Charmin shaman. I took a nosedive into rage. I had had *enough*.

I took a deep breath and considered my options. Should I walk upstairs, find more paper in the closet (where I store enough for a national disaster, which came in very handy during COVID-19), and replace the TP? Or . . .

It was time for Penn to figure this out. I snapped a damning picture of the empty roll and posted it with "???" on Instagram. Within hours, I had a thousand messages that said, "Oh my gosh, my family too!" and people started sharing their own pictures. The toilet paper standoff was *on*, friends. At the time, Penn didn't understand the workings of Instagram and had no idea what I was posting.

Over the next seven days, it was like *Gorillas in the Mist* set in our bathroom as I documented how my family either used the bathroom without toilet paper (*the horror*) or made the extra effort to walk upstairs to use a stocked potty. I got messages from women encouraging me to stand strong, saying "You got this!" and "We are here for you, Kim!" and "Don't ever give in."

They needn't have worried. If passive-aggressiveness were an Olympic sport, I would rep our country, and I would be up on that podium in that number one spot. I was in it to win it.

Finally, after a week—that is *seven days* in case you'd forgotten—someone alerted my husband to what was going on via social media. (Traitor. I'm warning you: I hold a grudge.) Who knows how long it would have lasted if they hadn't, or what would have happened when the *other* bathroom ran out of toilet paper . . .

PENN

I was upstairs, enjoying my morning quiet time on Twitter, when I saw a tweet saying "@pennholderness, she is *killing* you." That's all it said. *She's killing me?* What?

I looked through my feed, and there was nothing from my wife that made me suspicious. I went through Facebook—nothing. Finally, I remembered, *Oh, Instagram.* That's where Kim has her guerrilla platform. She knows that I would rather watch TikTok than look at Instagram stories, and I'm not an eleven-year-old girl. If my wife wanted to sneak attack without any fear of me knowing about it, Instagram was the place. Respect the player.

Once I got on Instagram, I figured out what the deal was pretty quickly. I mean, it's not like I hadn't noticed there was no toilet paper in the downstairs bathroom. It's just that I had been wiping my butt with Kleenex, which is way better than wiping with toilet paper. People who tell you it doesn't go down the drain are full of baloney. That's a racket invented by Big Toilet Paper. If you just use one or two tissues, you're gonna be fine. Let it sit there for a little bit, let it get softer, and you're golden.

If I'm being honest, I would have been happy to stay on the Kleenex train forever. Toilet paper is the worst. Even the sturdiest, most expensive brands do not get the job done and do not feel good. In the time since toilet paper was invented in 1857, we have invented basically everything—cars, planes, spaceships, Oreos—and we are cloning and 3D printing everything else. Yet somehow there have been no major advances in toilet paper technology in over a hundred years. Why can't toilet paper feel like facial tissue? I am inventing Toilet Paper That Feels Like Kleenex. Don't steal it.

But my cushy Kleenex well had run dry by this point, anyway. The day before I saw the Twitter message, the tissue box had disappeared. My last toilet appointment, I'd had to waddle into the kitchen with my pants down by my ankles, knees facing out, holding my butt cheeks apart the whole way until I could get a paper towel. It was nine o'clock in the morning, and our house is filled with windows. Any jogger or UPS driver happening by would have been scarred for the rest of their life. But I gotta tell you: paper towels—if they're good ones—are not bad.

The empty TP roll, the lack of tissues, and my early morning paper-towel tango were probably all signs that I should have gotten some more toilet paper. Instead, what I thought was, *Someone will put some more in there eventually.*

You know why I thought that? Because historically, if I waited long enough, the new roll of TP always showed up. I'd been batting a thousand for nearly a decade and a half. I'd been conditioned to expect it because that's what had always happened. Pavlov's dog started drooling when the bell rang because the food was *always there.*

When I saw the Instagram story, I made my way downstairs, all twitchy and embarrassed, and I said to Kim, "This is insane. What are you doing? Why couldn't you just tell me to replace the roll?"

The real answer probably was that she *had* said it—many, many times—but not loudly enough, and not with the definitive tone she decided to use when she responded to my question. Because Kim, God love her, is very binary with her emotions. She's patient, she's patient, she's patient . . . and then when something goes wrong, a switch flips. There's something called a wit's end; I don't know what it is, but she had reached it. She started in on how I don't ever do anything around the house.

She used *the world* against me, as in, "This is why the world was watching this, because this happens everywhere. The wives are left doing it all." She said this was just one small symptom of a bigger epidemic. There was no order, there was no respect, and she was the one left to shoulder all the work. All the time, always, forever.

Wait. What? I thought this was just about some two-ply paper. I know Kim does a lot around the house. I do. But let me give you a little backstory here.

I was a slob growing up. My mom told me to clean stuff up and I never did, and eventually she would do it for me. The same thing happened in college with my roommate—he always had a lower breaking point for the mess than I did, so he would eventually fold and clean up first. My job was to pay for pizza and to try to keep everyone in a good mood with my jokes. I felt like it evened out.

I've followed suit as an adult. The household situation is that I pay for pizza and I constantly tell my wife how much I love her. Plus anytime she asks me to do something, I stop what I'm doing and do it. Generally speaking.

You give me a sink full of dishes and I will do every single dish. I will wipe off every single countertop. I'm very good at cleaning up after parties because I'm tipsy and I can listen to music. Here's the thing, though: I'm very tall, so the ground is very far away from me. I've got bad knees, and I've got a bad back. The floor is a very distant, cold planet for me. Any time I pick anything up off the floor, I want a medal. I want someone (ahem, Kim) to walk into the room, clutch her hand to her heart, and say, "Penn Dameron Holderness, did you just pick up something I left on the floor? Praise be! Is it too late to ask Malala to share her award? 'Cause you, sir, are the true hero." I do change light bulbs—not when the first light bulb goes out, but when eight or nine light bulbs are not working. Doesn't that seem like a big enough contribution? Don't answer that. I know that's not enough. But that's what I do, and Kim handles the rest. I had no idea that the division of labor was bothering her so much.

I have no defense for the toilet paper incident, except that I didn't know it was a thing until my wife made it a national conversation (a very funny one at that, and I tip my hat to her). But how had TP become important enough that she felt she needed to deploy the social media nuclear option?

THE SECRET OF SECRET CONTRACTS

After we'd both cooled down—and Penn changed the toilet paper *on camera*—we did what we always do when we hit a roadblock in our marriage: we took it to Christopher. Christopher has a gift for helping us process our most baffling interactions. We gave him the poop. He sat back, listened in his patient, loving way that would be annoying if it weren't so welcoming, and then told us he knew exactly what was driving us up a wall.

Usually, when we tell Christopher about a fight we're having, he pulls back and helps us analyze what is going on underneath the words we're saying to each other. In this case, it was what we *weren't* saying that was throwing us for a loop. We were bumping into a phenomenon that is present in every relationship, one that undermines your ability to ask for what you want—even from the people you love. Maybe even *especially* from the people you love. Once you can spot it, you'll change the way you relate to your partner.

Christopher introduced us to the concept of *secret contracts*. Secret contracts are the silent deals you make with your partner by default and through routine. They are tasks we take on and identities we assume with an invisible handshake at the start of a relationship that we continue till death do us part—or until something happens that reveals the contract needs to be redlined.

When you first got together with your partner, each of you probably took on different responsibilities. You started chopping the vegetables; your partner started writing the grocery list. You started mowing the lawn; your partner knows who your internet provider is. You fell into these slots without thinking about it, and you never left.

Doesn't exactly get your heart racing, does it? Secret contracts are not sexy. In fact, they are as workaday and pedestrian as they come—but they do serve a purpose. Think about how exhausting it would be to have to negotiate every single aspect of our lives together afresh every day. We'd spend so much time talking and arguing that the dishes would pile up and bills would crowd the drawers. Towels would end up on the floor. (That disturbance you just felt was Kim shuddering.)

Secret contracts are universal. Every couple you've ever met has them. And they are not limited to romantic relationships. You have them with your mom and dad. You have them with your kids. You have them with your coworkers. Your mechanic. They have a place, but every once in a while, they need to be brought to the table for review.

BUT I NEVER SIGNED ANYTHING!

One of the reasons Penn quit his job as a sports anchor was so he could be more available for the kids. The first day he was free from his old 2:00 p.m. to midnight schedule, he volunteered to do the school runs. Every single morning since, he has driven the kids to school and sat in the long, long line to pick them up. (He has some very clear ideas for ways to improve drop-off efficiency if you care to hear them and have two hours.) But we never sat down and discussed this—he just did it. Penn adores this time with the kids. Because they are buckled in and can't escape, they are literally a captive audience, which is his dream. This is an example of a secret contract that works.

Other secret contracts can be dysfunctional, like the way Kim took on the lion's share of the housework early on in our marriage. From the beginning, the cooking, the grocery shopping, the meal planning, the laundry—that was all Kim. Paying bills, keeping track of the household activities, straightening up—you name it, she did it.

We didn't get married until Kim was twenty-nine, so she was used to taking care of things around the house. It wasn't like she was adding a bunch to what she was already doing, so it didn't even occur to her to do it another way—until it did.

Couples frequently dig grooves like this for themselves in relationships, and the deeper the groove, the harder it is to jump out of it. He's the caretaker; she's the good-time girl. She's rational; he's guided by instinct. We play those roles even when they no longer serve us because they have become habitual. When we are operating on autopilot, we let our behavior be guided by these roles instead of by our authentic desires, and that causes friction.

Identifying Your Secret Contracts

Once you know what secret contracts are, it's like looking for yellow cars: you see them everywhere. Here are a few questions to help you identify the secret contracts you have with your partner that might require a rewrite.

- What tasks do you do automatically, even if you don't have the time, energy, or desire to do them, simply because you have always done them? (Remember, your answer might not be a practical, get-'er-done–type responsibility. It may be that you are the default disciplinarian or the person who keeps the dinner conversation lively when the other guests are a snooze.)
- How often does assuming that responsibility make you feel resentful of your partner? Once a week? Once a day? Once an hour?
- Have you ever discussed those feelings with your partner?
- How often do you pretend to feel something you don't or feel pressured to respond in a particular way because it seems consistent with how other people view you?
- Does your partner know that you do so?
- How confident are you that your partner would understand if you asked for a change?

KIM

I had been *pumped* to talk to Christopher about our toilet paper standoff. I fully expected him to be 100 percent on my side. After all, I had thousands of women on the internet who agreed with me. How could I be wrong?

I wasn't wrong, per se, but Christopher showed me that my approach was. Looking at my TP shame bomb through the lens of a secret contract, I can see that when I was making a big, public, passive-aggressive brouhaha about the toilet paper, I didn't just want someone else to change the roll; I wanted to change *my role*.

For a long time, it had worked for us for me to be household manager. But when things started to take off with the videos, we were so focused on running that business that we didn't really talk through what it would mean for us as a family. Suddenly, we were running a business in which we were creating videos, podcasts, and blog posts at a dizzying rate. Penn is a mad scientist who can create a song in ten minutes, but 98 percent of the songs you see in our videos are my idea. They come from a very momcentric voice, and it requires some brain space to come up with them.

My brain works best when there's no clutter. I know, I know; there's all this evidence that mess actually spurs creativity, but those studies can suck it. I can't relax if there is a mountain of dishes in the sink or wet towels on the floor. My brain was full of organizing/scheduling/cleaning/replacing toilet paper; I needed that space and time back to be able to think. If we were going to make this work long-term, things needed to change.

After I sat down and examined the terms of our secret contract, I saw that I was spending four hours every Saturday doing domestic crap. I looked at my very capable family enjoying their Saturday, and I realized I didn't want to be the plate-spinning crazy person. I wanted time to think, and I wanted in on the fun.

I sat the family down and said, "Look, if you guys are going to suck for, let's see, 24 times 7 . . . 168 hours in a week, can I have one hour when that's not the case, when you agree to pitch in around the house and lighten my load?"

They conferred and decided, *Yeah, okay, this is literally the least we can do.*

So now we have a thing we call Power Hour on Saturdays. For one hour on Saturdays, we fix the stuff around the house. Of course, there were some eye rolls from the kids, but ultimately, they don't mind it, and Penn does like being told specifically how he can help because he wants to make me happy. We set a clock, crank up some music, and just go nuts on the chores. We go through the mail or fill out forms or clean the sink or order a new water filter or change the sheets or whatever. With four humans, you can get a lot done. It's like we're all on a team, which feels so much better than doing everything by myself.

Listen, it's not perfect. We're not perfect. It's a slow burn. My son thinks "Put away your laundry" means "Just cram as many pieces of clothing into one drawer as you possibly can." But it's better. I will look back on this one day and say, "I sure am glad I let my family fumble through cooking and cleaning because we are now all functioning members of society."

The best part is that now it's out in the open. Instead of quietly resenting my husband when the refrigerator is filthy, I'll show Penn the fridge and say, "Secret contract." There's a mountain of laundry everywhere? "Secret contract." There's an empty soap container? Can you say, "Secret contract?" Sure, there's a lot of rinse and repeat, but it doesn't feel like nagging; it feels like growing.

REWRITING A SECRET CONTRACT

There is nothing inherently wrong with having a role within a relationship. But problems can arise when one person wants to revise or broaden that role. Secret contracts become a more pressing issue when they move out of the realm of the practical day-to-day stuff and into identity and emotion territory, when you don't feel boxed in by what your partner expects you to do but by who they expect you to be.

It can be scary to break a secret contract. Routine is comforting, secure, and knowable. You know what works, so why change it? If it ain't broke and all. . . . And if it's not working, well, at least you've got a devil-you-know situation. It's easy to let your mental narrator tell you, *We've been living like this, but I'm scared that if I show my partner what I really want, they might feel like it's a breach of contract. What if their love was predicated on a contract that says I am spontaneous or frugal or kind? What if I also want to be predictable or generous or sarcastic? Will they walk?* The problem is that most of the roles we play represent only a part of who we are.

Maybe you've heard the parable about the blind men and the elephant. As the story goes, six blind men lived in a village in India where other villagers cared for them. The men spent their days engaged in deep discussions with one another about the world. One day, they started talking about elephants, as you do eventually when you've been talking to the same five people day in and day out for most of your life. Before long, they were arguing about the nature of an elephant. Their argument grew so heated, so noisy, that it was driving the rest of the villagers nuts. They told the men, "Stop your fighting! You want an elephant? We'll show you an elephant."

They arranged to take the men to the palace, where there was an elephant on the grounds. A villager led the first blind man to the elephant, and the man touched the animal's trunk. "An elephant is like a snake," he declared. "It is pliable and can bend and weave with ease." When it was the second man's turn, he placed his hand on the creature's tusk, and he said, "Ah! An elephant is very smooth, like rock that has been polished." The third man, having touched the elephant's ear, told the assembled crowd, "No, my friends are mistaken. An elephant is floppy and covered with coarse hairs." The other three men took their turns, and each came to a different conclusion about the nature of an elephant, depending on where their hands had landed on the beast. They began arguing anew, their shouts growing so loud that they summoned the raja, who came into the courtyard. When the crowd hushed, the raja pointed out that an elephant was in fact a very large creature with many different characteristics, and the men had each come to know only a very small part of it.

At any given time, we each show only a small part of our elephants to our partners. We might think we know our partners inside and out—we might even use that as a measure of how successful our relationship is—but the truth of the human condition is it is impossible to know each other fully. We have a friend who is the most loyal, compassionate person on the planet. He's the type who not only remembers your birthday but sends a long note recalling a memory he really cherishes about you . . . just because. But put Brad on the tennis court, and a whole other side of him comes roaring out. He is fierce, maybe too fierce. He never turns it on other people—even his doubles partner—but he says the most hateful things about himself. The woman who is now his wife had dated him for three years before she ever watched him play and had a chance to see that side of him, and it was a shock. Fortunately, she had built up stores of good feelings toward him and had the sense to recognize that his anger on the court was not affecting their relationship, so she didn't let it spook her. But it was a surprise because he had been exquisitely careful not to let her see that side of him for most of their courtship.

We know only what the other person chooses to show us. On the flip side, we make choices about what we ourselves will show our partners. When we see the people we love enjoying one part of us, it is tempting to keep presenting that aspect of ourselves again and again for their approval. *Here! Here is my tusk, nice and smooth, just as it's always been!* We bend and contort so that our partners never end up with a handful of snot. But you are so much more than any single part. People are complex not only because are we multifaceted but also because we are constantly growing and changing. This can make for some scary moments when we want to show a new part of ourselves, because what if we do that and our partners don't like what they find? Some parts are pretty raw.

PENN

What Christopher said about secret contracts hit me deep when I realized that they applied to stuff that was bigger than a chore wheel. The first thing that came to mind was a contract that's been in place in our relationship for as long as I can remember. I don't need to tear it up and write a new one, but I might need to draft an amendment.

We have a contract that states that I am the official Mood Keeper-Upper in our relationship. Kim calls me a golden retriever, and it is true that I'm generally very happy-go-lucky and eager to help. I love to tell jokes and keep people smiling. Also, I'm happiest when I'm fetching things or being rubbed.

Admittedly, it's not *just* that I like to keep people happy. I also *really* like attention. My dad told me that I came into the world waiting for applause. If I can get someone to laugh or to clap or to smile, that is my definition of awesome. Nothing's better. Someone once bought me a T-shirt that read "Look at me" across the chest. It was a perfect fit.

KIM

There's a reason golden retrievers are such popular dogs. They are delightful. This guy I married—he is the funniest person in the room, and he is the happiest person in the room. He makes me laugh a genuine laugh several times daily. Not a giggle or a snort; a *laugh*. This can be a problem because I've had two kids and if I laugh too hard, well, I might need a costume change.

Penn wants everyone to have a good time all the time, and he's willing to do what it takes to make it happen—like he did at my cousin Jen's wedding. It was a beautiful event. And as at most weddings, no one wanted to be the first on the dance floor. We needed the party starter. We needed the hype man. Cue Penn Holderness. I have often joked that if people stop watching our videos, I'm going to pay for the kids' college tuition by renting him out for bar mitzvahs. Most people have hemoglobin in their blood. Penn has hype-oglobin.

At Jen's wedding, he ran out onto the dance floor like a champ. He was giving it his all—leaning back, teaching people how to dougie, and chicken noodle souping all over creation . . . by himself. I shouldn't have worried though. Next thing I knew, he had taken my grandmother's hand and pulled her to the dance floor. My grandmother is my hero, and she was a total sport—except she was wearing these little tiny heels, and as she was dancing, she started to fall. This was not the first time Penn has had to save someone who was falling on the dance floor, so he was all, *No big deal, I got this*, and he bent to catch her. But something happened with her trajectory, and suddenly it was very clear he wasn't going to be able to heave her back up before she landed. Instead he just laid her ever so gently onto the ground.

Once she was down there, he looked at her and he said, "Mema!

Tuck your knees!" And she was like, "What?" She is a proper lady after all.

Everybody was staring at them. I thought Jen was going to expire.

Penn shouted again, "Tuck your knees to your chest!" So Mema tucked her knees to her chest, and Penn took her, and he spun her around, so she did three back spins like a top in a tasteful chiffon dress. When Mema finished spinning, Penn lifted her and she jumped up. The crowd went wild. *Party. Started.*

That wedding was three months before we got married, so if I had had any doubts that this was the guy whose wagon I wanted to be hitched to for all of eternity, that epic save on the dance floor sealed the deal. It was Penn to the core—fun-loving, selfless, and eager to please.

PENN

True as that may be, I married a woman who has struggled with depression. So on top of my natural inclination to please, over the years I have come to consider it my job to be the fun person and the bringer of cheer because there are times when the chemicals in Kim's body just take over. I feel like it's my responsibility to be up all the time.

Here's where the secret contract makes things tricky: because I am the golden retriever, I feel like I am supposed to be happy with whatever bone is in front of me no matter what else is going on in my life. It can be a lot to handle because sometimes I get down too. I have had really, truly sad moments that feel like a female period times twenty. On top of that, I've recently started getting some pretty terrific little panic attacks. But when I start to slip into sadness, I don't stop and look at what's going on; I'm much more concerned with making sure everyone around me is happy.

When we plan a visit to Kim's family, she tells me, "I get so anxious visiting such a large, spread-out family. I can't go on these trips without you." It gives me great joy to be able to help in any way that I can because I know dealing with divorced parents and making multiple stops can be complicated. But when I'm at the end of my rope, I feel like I can't really say, "Hey, Kim, when we're with your family, can you please stop expecting that I'm going to be the life of the party for seven straight days?"

Because being the life of the party is my best thing. That's a big part of why we work. I always thought that if I wanted to revise that contract, she'd walk away thinking, *There goes the fun guy that I married*. What if she looked at me and said, "Well, what is it that you're good for, then?"

TAKING THE RISK

When we break a secret contract, we're revising terms that have long worked for us. Revising a secret contract requires vulnerability. Sometimes it seems easier to let a contract remain protectively in place than to reveal what we really want because revealing ourselves can be frightening. We wear clothes because showing our bodies to just anyone is too intimate. We don't cry at work because crying is considered a sign of vulnerability. The question you ask when you allow yourself to be vulnerable is "Will you still love me if I show you this sensitive, private part of me?"

But to create a trusting relationship, we must have faith that our partners will love our whole selves, not just one tiny part. This is the real holy grail of marriage, a feeling of safety and security that stems from knowing that your partner will love you even if you show them your full and ever-changing self.

KIM

I have a perfect example of a time when I could tell Penn was wagging his tail when part of him wanted to be curled up in a ball.

Penn does not find value in being sad. My brain will spiral like a corkscrew at the first sign of trouble (*it's not a cold, it's pneumonia; it's not pneumonia, it's lung cancer—the contagious kind*). Penn's brain isn't programmed to do that. He doesn't take a deep dive just to be sad, because what good is that going to do anybody? But after fifteen years of marriage, I can tell when our golden retriever is sad because he gets really quiet, and Penn is rarely quiet.

His mom has a pretty advanced level of dementia that has developed and presented itself over the course of a decade. For the first half of it, her fully capable and coherent husband could help out with it, but his dad has since started slipping himself.

It got to a point about two years ago that Penn knew he had to tell his parents they needed to leave their home. His mom needed around-the-clock care, and she needed to be away from his dad because he was her crutch—and not necessarily her nurse. There's a reason why it's called *skilled* nursing.

That's hard to say to your parents. Now imagine *Penn*, the happy-go-lucky, make-everyone-smile guy, doing it.

PENN

Kim's right. Dealing with aging parents has definitely taxed my ability to stay upbeat.

I'll tell you something: having a parent with Alzheimer's is *not* easy, just as the way dealing with an unpredictable nation-state is not easy. One of the hardest parts is that I've had to find new ways to relate to my mother. When you have Alzheimer's, you revert to your teenage self. Or maybe your twenty-year-old self. God help my kids if this happens to me. They had best pray there is a beer pong table in my care facility. This Benjamin Button thing keeps going, so you get to your ten-year-old self, two-year-old self, and then you can't talk and you can barely walk, and you certainly can't take care of yourself. Right now, my mom can move around, she can eat, she can go to the bathroom. She knows who I am, but she doesn't remember my name. She can't finish a sentence. That's been hard on this happy dog.

Just as things were getting really rough, Kim sat me down and said the magic words: "Secret contract." She told me that it was her turn to be the good-mood dude. Or at least I didn't have to play that role when I wasn't feeling it. I wish I could say I was immediately like, "You got yourself a deal, lady," and that I let her take over the mood-regulating in the household from that moment forward. It wasn't quite like that, but I didn't make a joke about it right away either. She was giving me permission to show her a new part of my elephant, and that felt pretty terrific. (Not that part. Gross.)

One day when I was visiting my mom, I brought over my guitar on a whim. I have my mom to thank for a lot of my musical ability. I took lessons, of course, but I didn't really pay attention to them. (I know. You're shocked.) Where I really learned about music was sitting next to her at the piano in our basement, starting around fourth grade. She would have been in her forties then. Slender and almost six feet tall, she was like a pretty giraffe with Andrew Jackson's hair. What can I say? It was the eighties; she had a perm.

Mom was a preacher's wife, and she had spent months of Sundays singing hymns. She would sit next to me and sing or hum "Onward, Christian Soldiers" or "The Water Is Wide" or "Blest Be the Tie that Binds," and then she'd wait for me to fumble them out on the keyboard, like a musical Simon Says. When I got good at that, she would just hum random notes, six or seven of them, and I'd play them back, then try to bring in accompaniment with chords underneath and turn it into an actual song. She was training my ear. To this day, I can't read music, but I can hear a song and just play it.

So when I brought out the guitar during that visit and started strumming, I played "Onward, Christian Soldiers." I thought she might get a kick out of it; maybe I'd get her to smile. I was like five notes in when she joined in, not just singing, but coming in on a major third above what I was singing. The nurses were like, "What the hell?" It was amazing.

Now, every time I go to visit my mom—either with the rest of the family or by myself—I bring my guitar. The feeling of connecting with her again is 90 percent joy, but I have to tell you, the other 10 percent is rough. There's guilt because I'm not able to do it every day, and there's also the worry about whether I'm looking in a mirror that's reflecting me a couple decades down the road. I try to feel the joy, but I also try to sit with that other 10 percent sometimes. Exploring this side of myself doesn't feel natural, but it feels right. I'm getting to know a new part of me. I'm hoping I'll grow from it, and I trust Kim will still love me when I do—as long as I remember to change the toilet paper.

Revising a Secret Contract

The good news is that revising a secret contract doesn't have to be an earthquake for your relationship. Done right, it can help you to live more authentically and with more trust in your partner.

How you make your request is just as important as what you

actually say. When you recognize that you have something to ask your partner, especially something that will change the terms of a secret contract, here's how you do it in a way that promotes intimacy:

Wait for the right time. Negotiate during peacetime, not in the heat of battle. Set aside a time when you won't be distracted—no cell phones or kids or radio on in the background. Sit with a glass of wine or cup of tea on the couch, or agree to go on a walk.

Use words of invitation. Invite your partner to join you by saying, "Do you have a minute? There's something on my mind I need to talk to you about."

Finish with gratitude. After you've had your conversation, thank your partner. Tell them, "Thank you for listening to me. I feel closer to you now."

It can be tricky to know how to start this conversation, so we have come up with a few prompts for you to think about before you have a talk. You might want to write your answers down on a piece of paper and share them with your partner beforehand, so they have time to absorb them.

Our secret contract says:
How I think you see me:
How I wish you would see me:
This contract has been working for me in these ways:
It no longer works for me because:
I would love to revisit these aspects of it:
If this part doesn't change, I can live with it:
I haven't brought this up with you before because:
Changing this will help me to:

05

I'M STRUGGLING WITH SNUGGLING

THE FIGHT

KIM

One night in the early days of our relationship, we were at a dinner party with a few married couples. Balancing my plate of appetizers in one hand and a full glass of chardonnay in the other, I joined a pair of women by the fireplace just as one of them said, "I pretend to be asleep when he comes into bed at night." The other one nodded conspiratorially and chimed in, "I tell him my period lasts for fourteen days, and he doesn't question it." When I realized they were talking about ways to avoid sex with their husbands, I coughed up a shrimp and spilled my wine down my shirt. (Note: I really need to work on my poker face.) They looked at me, eyes full of pity, and said in unison, "Just wait until you're married."

I gave a half-hearted giggle, but I thought to myself smugly, *Whatever you say, ladies. I will never, ever not want to rip Penn's clothes off.*

To be fair, I was basing that on our track record. Penn and I had known each other for around ten months at that point. That whole time, the physical affection was off the charts. We couldn't keep our hands off each other. In private, in public; it didn't matter—we were drawn to each other by an irresistible force. I'm sure we made some people throw up in their mouths when they saw us together.

After dating for about a year, we got engaged, and then we got married nine months later. Not long after our wedding, we were living in a tiny apartment in Manhattan. I was a correspondent for *Inside Edition* and Penn was working for ABC Sports, and I came down with a sinus infection I couldn't kick. It was one of those stubborn infections where I woke up with pressure under my eyes, which I only managed to forget about when the headache I'd get each day became bad enough to distract me. My doctor wrote me a prescription, but even after I got on antibiotics, I was feeling nauseous and everything smelled terrible. I went back to the doctor thinking I had some sort of secondary infection, but then he asked, "Is there a chance you could be pregnant?" *Wut?* I was on the pill, so I'd thought I was covered, but I took a test just to be sure. Actually, I took nine—*nine!*—tests. I wanted to be really sure. You know that big yellow sticker on the antibiotics bottle with bold text that says, "ANTIBIOTICS RENDER BIRTH CONTROL PILLS COMPLETELY USELESS. IF YOU INSIST ON HAVING SEX WHILE YOU'RE SICK, YOU WILL GET KNOCKED UP"? Yeah. That's a real thing.

I was, in fact, pregnant. We were overjoyed, but surprised.

Penn was one of those husbands who was bizarrely turned on

by seeing his wife gain weight. My butt was as wide as the broad side of a school bus, but he loved it. Pregnancy didn't slow down our sex life at all.

Then came our sweet Lola. Suddenly, our world turned completely, totally, utterly upside down. She didn't sleep, so neither did we. She screamed and wailed whenever we put her down, so we rarely did. (We were first-time parents. Don't judge us, Karen.) She nursed all the time but wasn't gaining enough weight, so when her crying wasn't keeping us awake, worrying about her was. My body? Well, let's just say items shifted during flight. My deflated stomach looked like a saggy, sad water balloon. I had a screaming baby clawing at my sore boobs 24/7. My whole person was swollen and puffy. There was never a time when a tiny human wasn't hanging off me. I was overtired and overtouched. In the very few moments when I wasn't holding our baby, I didn't want to touch anyone else, and that included Penn.

Most of our nights went something like this: work for an hour to get Lola to sleep, smear toothpaste on our teeth, dump clothes in a pile on the floor, fumble into bed, and pray the baby didn't wake up. The idea of having sex was as unfathomable as breathing underwater.

I knew Penn was unhappy with this arrangement, and he wasn't alone. I wanted to want sex again. If not for my sake, for Penn's. He'd still nuzzle my neck as I was washing out bottles and try to pull me close as I was folding receiving blankets. At night, he'd bust out his signature move—the please-let-this-lead-to-sex back rub—but instead of relaxing when he'd reach over to touch my shoulders, I would think, *Oh, God. Please, no*, and then squeeze my eyes shut tight and try to drool on my pillow a little to signal that I was asleep until he'd give up and roll back over to his side of the bed. As I was playing possum one night, I realized, *OMG, I'm one of those women who pretends to be asleep to avoid sex!*

PENN

It's not like I can't tell when Kim is faking sleep. I happen to know that she has the hearing of a werewolf. If I even *think* about moving an inch of our comforter to my side of the bed, she can hear it. She can sense the crack of light under the door when someone turns on a light *in another room*. There is no way she was too conked out to feel my back rubs. I got the message loud and clear: she did not want to have sex with me.

This was a rude surprise because, as Kim said, in the beginning was the sex, and the sex was good and the good was sex. Through sex, all things were made. It seemed like every conversation we had back then ended up with us being naked. It was like, "Did you get milk at the . . . well, hello!" (Cue saxophone.) We were like firecrackers going off, *pop pop pop pop pop*. My formula for getting in the mood was pretty much: *I look at her, she looks great . . . let's do this!* To put it bluntly, it was *awesome*.

But then the fireworks fizzled. Yes, we still had incredibly intimate moments in the quiet of our humble home, but it was a different type of intimacy that didn't involve touching. Full disclosure: I didn't love that kind of intimacy. It felt like the equivalent of shopping the as-is aisle at IKEA—theoretically great, but actually busted and disappointing. I couldn't stop wondering, *Why aren't we having sex? Why, why, why, why, why, why?*

I tried everything I could think of to get things back on track. I rocked my best Tim Riggins smolder. Nothing. I flexed my triceps. Nada. I feigned disinterest, hoping a hard-to-get routine would come through for me. Nope. I thought, *Okay, now I see what's happening. She's having some issues about her body after childbirth. I'm going to wait patiently for her to feel better about herself. Being a good dude will probably make me more desirable.* I kept myself occupied with crossword puzzles and endless podcasts. Anytime I was in bed at night beside her and I wanted to have sex, instead of reaching over, I'd ask myself, *How many Atlanta Braves can you name? Can you name a hundred?* I'd start naming them—*Ozzie Albies, Johan Camargo, Ender Inciarte*—until I fell asleep. (For the record, I could get to eighty-five.)

I gave her enough space to park an Escalade.

Now, this is going to get kinda personal. The few times we had actually got around to having sex, the encounters, well, they weren't great. I could tell Kim was going through the motions without much enthusiasm—and that was not good for my confidence, to put it mildly. So one night, when she rolled onto my side of the bed and let her foot touch mine, which she *never* does unless she is open to having sex, I thought to myself, *This is going to end badly.* Now, if you're a guy, and you think *This is going to end badly*, it's going to end badly, so instead of reacting with the eagerness of Scooby-Doo, I gave her a peck on the cheek, skootched over so our feet were no longer touching, and then grabbed a book and started studying it like it contained a treasure map.

Next thing I knew, the bed was shaking. Not with passion—my wife was a bucket of sobs.

LET ME HEAR YOUR BODY TALK

We both knew that things were not okay with our physical relationship, but we were too chicken to say anything about it. (Can you say *stonewalling*?) Why was it such a hard conversation to have?

We know we were not alone when we were skipping sex. We've heard it said that one in seven couples in the US is living in a sexless marriage. That sounds like a national crisis to us. We want to help.

It might seem weird that we are giving you advice about getting your sex life on track in a book about communication, but hear us out. Sex *is* a form of communication. In psychologist Albert Mehrabian's famous studies on nonverbal communication, he found than more than 50 percent of communication came from body language. We say so much with our bodies, even when giving a presentation or watching a baseball game on the couch, but our body language speaks loudest when it comes to sexual attraction.

When we have sex, we drop the barriers, literal and figurative, between ourselves and our partners. You're literally naked. Your partner gets to see what you've got going on under your clothes, sure, but they also get to see what's under all the social niceties and good manners we layer on top of our most primal, animalistic selves. When we lift the latch on the cage and let those creatures out into the wild, it is both exhilarating and terrifying. Trusting someone enough to show them the side of you that yelps and squirms is a big deal. When someone has seen your inner beast and still sticks around, it creates a strong bond.

As with most things, there is a biochemical explanation for this feeling. When you have sex with your partner, your brain releases a chemical called oxytocin, commonly referred to as the love hormone, which bonds you to your partner. It also stimulates the release of dopamine, which causes the reward center of your brain to light up like a Christmas tree when you are in your partner's presence. This one-two punch creates a kind of halo effect around your partner. Your brain gets conditioned to think *Ohhhh, good things happen around this person—more please!* It's not for nothing that we call it *making love*.

When your sex life has gone off the rails, you've lost an important way to generate those warm, fuzzy feelings that lead to intimacy and connection. Lack of sexual connection leads to lack of emotional and spiritual connection, which is certainly what happened during our dry spell. We were short with each other. We didn't seek each other out during the day. We turned inward instead of reaching out to each other.

When you are not having sex, it can feel like your partner is saying something bigger and more painful than "I'm not interested in sex." It can feel like a one-person referendum on whether you are worth being around.

We're not trying to stress you out or make you feel like you are a failure if you're not going at it day and night—after all, desire can ebb and flow, and what feels like enough sex for one couple might be the Sahara Desert of intercourse for another—but every couple requires some degree of physical intimacy for real connection. Christopher refers to sex as a "marriage marker," a reasonable hope, activity, and aspect of marriage that can serve as an indicator of how healthy a relationship is.

This might be obnoxious to say, but with a few exceptions since that postbaby downtime, we've had a pretty good sex life. Before you get to hating us, we want to share the counterintuitive secret to our success with you so you can turn that ship to Sexless Marriage Island around. We're going to identify the obstacles, give you the world's least sexy solution to good sex, and then throw you a sexy little curveball.

We recently had Cindy Eckert, CEO of the Pink Ceiling—which makes Addyi, known as the female Viagra—on our podcast. She shared an incredible statistic with us: If you are in a relationship and you're having great sex, it will add 20 percent to your relationship value. If you're not having great sex, it will reduce the value by 70 percent. Isn't that astonishing? As Cindy said, "If it breaks down in the bedroom, it breaks down at the breakfast table." Amen to that.

The thing is, most of the relationship advice we've encountered over the years suggests that if something isn't crackling in the bedroom, you'll need to fix everything else that's wrong with your relationship to get your sex life back on track. Erm. We beg to differ. In our experience, that has not been the case. In fact, we'd humbly like to suggest the exact opposite: get busy, and everything else will get better.

PENN

I cannot tell you how true this is for me. If I go, like, five days without sex, I get moody. We are talking pouty—sit-in-my-room-and-lie-on-the-bed-until-someone-comes-in-and-asks-me-what's-wrong-and-hopefully-also-has-sex-with-me pouty. The world, which seemed really great a few days ago, doesn't seem that great anymore. Everything seems dimmer, like when your phone adjusts its brightness when you move into a dark room. After I let out enough aggressive sighs, Kim will ask me flat out, "What's wrong?" and even though something is clearly wrong, I'll say, "Nothing," and go back to moping.

This goes on for a while until I finally break down and say to her, "You know what, every once in a while, I just wonder if I'm doing the right thing, and I don't feel confident, and I don't feel like I'm enough." She'll look at me, and she'll be like, "Do you want to have sex?" And nine times out of ten that sets things right again. I feel happier about myself, happier about Kim, and happier about our lives in general.

THE THREE DS

If we both knew that sex made everything better, then why weren't we having more of it? During our sex drought and our accompanying filibuster, we had fallen victim to what Christopher calls *the three Ds*:

distraction (Let's talk about or do something—anything—else), denial (Problem? What problem?), and delay (We can deal with this later; there's plenty of time). These three specters appear during stress points in relationships. When they do, they can paralyze couples' sex lives.

Let's start with distraction. Part of the reason we weren't having more sex was because we were so busy doing everything else. We don't need to tell you how crowded and full of distraction life can be. Right now, we are in what Christopher calls the carpool stage of life. We have two kids, but it seems like they're doing eight kids' worth of activities. It's like we're air traffic control, and we're trying to land everything safely in a storm while we're short-staffed.

Here is a typical Holderness family to-do list:

- Pack lunches
- Grocery shop
- Write blog post
- Schedule podcast guest for next week
- Marketing plan for Well Body Reset
- Buy wigs
- Haircuts for kids
- Dentist appointment, all
- Orangetheory Fitness class
- Script for next video
- Gutter guy
- Yard guy
- HVAC guy
- Car guy
- Vet appointment for Sunny

Your list probably looks similar. (What do you mean you don't have "buy wigs" on yours?) Is it any wonder sex gets bumped off the agenda?

When she was on the podcast, Cindy Eckert told us something really interesting about sexual desire: it is linked to your ability to relax. Apparently, for some people, primarily women, it is impossible for their brains to shut off. Researchers even did brain scans and the images showed that women with low sexual desire had highly active brains. For women who are type A, who have fast information processing, their brains aren't quieting down enough for them to hear their inner animals begging to be released.

KIM

When I heard Cindy talk about this, it gave me goosebumps.

It made so much sense to me. You can't be in a sexy state of mind if you have a mental track on loop saying, "Okay, so tomorrow that permission slip needs to go in her book bag, and PC has basketball at four o'clock. How many times have I given them hummus for lunch already this week? I need to remember that my in-laws' furniture needs to be . . ."

There is *always* something else demanding your attention. The gym, the walk, the book, or probably the biggest boner crusher of anything on the planet, your phone.

Distractions escalate when you're a parent and you're tasked with keeping another human alive. It's consuming. I've seen this happen with so many couples—they've stopped talking about themselves and only talk about the kids.

In our case, when we had our sex standoff, we were also dealing with postpartum depression and a colicky baby. It led to a total shutdown. We had let the distractions pile up so high that they buried the problem. We were in *denial*.

It was as if sex had become the equivalent of going to the dentist: something I wasn't really looking forward to but knew I needed to do in order to keep things healthy. Yet I was willing to *delay* that appointment indefinitely. It was like, "My teeth are fine. I just brushed them five days ago. They're okay."

WILL YOU STILL LOVE ME TOMORROW?

So, great. Let's just all have more sex and then everything will be all sunshine and roses. The problem is that it's not always easy to keep the desire to have sex with your partner blazing as the years pass. You know how they say that the brain is your most powerful sex organ? It's true. Desire starts when you tune in to what excites you about your partner—long before you get horizontal.

In long-term relationships, there is a tension between what is familiar and what is exciting. Think back to the beginning of your relationship. Everything about your partner felt interesting, and you hung on their every word. They could have described a traffic jam and you'd be like, "And *then* what did that Acura do? Turn without signaling? No! Do go on . . ." In those early days, your brain is swimming in dopamine, the hormone that activates your pleasure center, because novelty stimulates its release. You get a hit of pleasure when you discover something—or someone—new. It's delightful.

Your partner has chosen you as the person they want to spend the most time with of anyone else of the 7.7 billion people on the planet. They've promised to stick with you through your snort snores and your Gumby dancing at weddings. That feels good. But after you've been courting awhile, the law of diminishing returns kicks in, and you raise the bar a little on what holds you rapt. You get accustomed to each other's charms, and that good feeling comes around less often. The change feels . . . not good. The fear that you will no longer hold your partner's attention and interest is the worst.

The absolute worst. When you feel uncertain about your ability to attract your mate, it can be wicked destabilizing.

As much fun as it would be to feel blown away by every single thing your partner says and does for all of eternity, it's simply not sustainable. You need to redirect some of that mental energy to working and eating and paying the Verizon bill. Getting back to a state of neutral-to-appreciative feelings about your partner is only natural, but it can still sting when you realize your partner is no longer spending all of their time thinking about you.

PENN

When Kim was around eight months pregnant with Lola, she looked at me and said, "Promise me that after this baby comes, we will still be each other's favorite." *Boy, did I ever marry the right woman*, I thought as I hugged her and promised her it would be the case.

Now, I would willingly contract smallpox and the plague at the same time if it meant my children would live a slightly happier life. My love for them burns brighter than a thousand suns, so I know what I'm about to say is not a good look for me . . . but I miss being the center of attention. When it was just the two of us, I got so much attention! I love attention! I was the center of Kim's universe back then, but orbits shifted when two new celestial bodies joined us, and I felt my gravitational pull lessen.

In the years since the kids were born, I have gone pretty darn gray. My lower back hurts constantly, my knees ache, I can't sleep on my left shoulder, and every time I look down at the shower drain there is a little clump of hair staring me in the face, saying, "It's over, man."

I'm really glad Kim thinks I'm funny, but there is a teenage boy inside me who wants her first thought about me to be, *Daaaaaamnnnn, my man is smoking hot*. I know too well the horror of looking in the mirror and knowing this is the best I will ever look again. And, yes, yes, I know Kim isn't going to leave me for the pool boy (we don't have a pool, suckers!), but when I see a thirty-year-old who can bench twice what I can, man, it is humbling. I remind myself that I have a family who loves me even though I routinely tell dad jokes and do goofy dances in front of millions of people, but sometimes, I would like it if heads turned when I walk into a room. Not because they are trying to figure out where they've seen me before, but because I'm a frigging sex magnet. I know Kim feels insecure sometimes, too, which is crazy to me because she is about a hundred times more beautiful now than she was when I first met her. But try telling her that.

Even though one of her love languages is words of affirmation, there are times when I tell her that she looks really nice in something, and she'll be like, "No, my butt looks huge." Then an hour later, the checkout girl at Trader Joe's will say it to her, and she'll be like, "Oh my gosh, thank you so much! That makes me feel amazing." My wife doesn't take any stock in what I say to her anymore. I've become white noise.

KIM

I am definitely guilty of tuning Penn out when he compliments me. Please, I own a mirror. I know I look like a troll when I wake up. Before I've had my coffee I'm puffy all over. I have dark circles under my eyes that look like one of the kids socked me while we were wrestling. I know we're lucky to live long enough to grow old, but I am not into the fact that it feels like my face is sliding off of my skull. Penn will still grab my butt and be like, "Hello, gorgeous." Is he serious? Listen, no one wants to think of themselves as superficial, but it is so incredibly hard to shake the idea that if I don't keep it tight, I won't matter anymore—to society and, geez, I hate to admit this, even to Penn. I take care of myself. I eat well, I work out, I am a boss about sleep. But Father Time is a cruel master, so it's hard to take Penn's sweet nothings to heart when my hair is in forty-seven different directions.

GETTING FRESH

You've probably experienced this ability to discount the nice things your partner says about you too. The first time your partner whispers, "You smell sexy" in your ear, you flush with pleasure. By the fiftieth time, you're like, "Meh, that's probably the barbeque smoke in my hair." We are programmed to take delight in novelty, and yet at the same time, we're creatures of habit. We make the same jokes at parties, we have a regular coffee order, and we tend to give the same compliments to our partners again and again.

Christopher is a huge proponent of taking the time to notice positive things about your partner. In an attempt to turn the white noise back into white heat, we each came up with five things we appreciate about each other now that we didn't know about when we met.

Penn:

1. I didn't know how funny you were.
2. You have really, really nice legs. I didn't spend a lot of time looking at them back in the day—my attention was elsewhere—but they're very sexy.
3. You are super tough. You gave birth to two children *and* you got punched in the face during the swim portion of a triathlon and kept going.
4. You're a better cook than you think you are.

5. You don't give a bleep. It's not that you don't care—you're very caring—but the small stuff, the drama, the little things don't get you down.

Kim:

1. You are really motivated about everything, from working out to eating right to getting work done.
2. I find it really sweet that you take care of your aging parents, singing to your mom and taking your dad for groceries every Friday.
3. You are a much better listener fifteen years later.
4. I knew you were like a cruise director, but I didn't quite realize what a special gift it was that you could make our entire family and anyone around you laugh.
5. I love your gray hair. It's sexy to be with somebody long enough to see their hair turn gray.

Reading these lists gave us a fun jolt of that "Hey, baby, whatchu about?" feeling. It was fantastic.

Be a Freshmaker

To light up those pleasure centers in your partner's brain, switch up your compliments. Write down five things that you have learned about your partner since you first started dating and then hand each other your lists. Try to be as specific as possible. "You are loyal" is good, but "When you stood up for me in front of your uncle at Thanksgiving, I was ready to excuse myself and head upstairs to your childhood bedroom" is better.

The great thing about this exercise is that it reminds you what's awesome about your partner, and then you get to feel incredible when you hear what they find awesome about you. Bring on the dopamine.

KIM

Back to our (temporarily) sexless marriage. The lack of connection in the bedroom was spilling over into the rest of our lives. I was avoiding *my own husband*, my forever guy. If I was ever going to have sex again, I needed to break through my stone wall and say something. Finally, I sat Penn down and said, "Penn, we aren't having enough sex. It's a problem."

Penn practically started panting and said he'd be willing to sell all of his personal possessions for more time together in the sack.

The relief I felt was enormous. We hadn't even touched each other, and already I felt more connected to him. If I had known what a difference it was going to make, I would not have delayed so long.

Something I will occasionally hear from a friend who is having a sex slowdown with their partner is "Once we have moved into our new place" or "Once the kids are back in school . . ." They're putting off fixing an essential part of their relationship until whatever stage of life they're in ends. But there's never going to be a perfect time to start focusing on your sex life. You have to just do it.

Have a Quickie

When was the last time you talked about your sex life with your partner?

That's what we thought.

Chances are, you've discussed the best way to load the dishwasher more recently than whether you are having the amount of sex you'd both like. It's time for that to change.

This is one of those jump-in-the-pool situations. You might not want to do it, but the faster you do it, the better. Don't make it a long, painful ease-into-the-water process. Make it quick, like a surgical strike. Give yourself five minutes and ask your partner these two questions:

1. Are we doing it as much as you'd like?
2. How often would you do it in an ideal world?

And then give your answers. This is not the time to talk through your body issues or your favorite position; just get it out there. Pin it down with words, and then go back to brushing your teeth.

IT MIGHT NOT BE SEXY, BUT IT WORKS

Naming the problem is half the battle. But it's only the first half. If you want to get into shape, you can't just say "I'm going to run on the treadmill." You have to actually get your butt on the machine and start sweating.

Christopher asked us to do a time survey to drive home the point that if we weren't making time for each other, *we weren't making time for each other.* If we wanted romance to blossom again, we had to make space and time for it.

Making sex a priority meant doing the least sexy thing you can imagine: putting it on our schedule. We know what you're thinking—you guys, there is a reason that none of those erotic movies (which you have never, ever watched and neither have we) begin with dialogue like this:

"Hey, I would like some intimate time. How about tonight after the kids' basketball game?"

"Sounds great, but I don't know. I'm slow-cooking a brisket, and I'll need to take it out around then."

"Well, can you fit in some time at 4:15?"

"Sure! In the meantime, I'm going to go around the house and pick up glasses full of half-drunk liquids."

But, nevertheless, we scheduled sex as if it were a doctor's appointment.

PENN

Yep, we got on our Google Calendars and looked at what would work for us, the same way we'd schedule a time when we'd both be able to meet with our accountant. We agreed that we were so exhausted by dealing with colic that we were spent by nightfall, so we'd have to make time to get busy first thing in the morning. On the appointed day, we checked our Google invites, and turned to each other with big, fat grins on our faces. It was a good way to start the day, and it set the tone for the rest of it.

The hilarious thing is that we made it even less sexy by coming up with the code word *laundry*. So to this day, on our calendar, between "shopping" and "dinner with Byrd and Alanna" we'll have a forty-five–minute slot for *laundry*. It might not be hot, but scheduling allows for anticipation instead of uncertainty. It guarantees that we will connect even during a busy week. The only downside is that sometimes, Kim will say, "Hey, we should fold the laundry."

I'll drop whatever I'm doing and run upstairs, and then when I get to the bedroom, there are, like, six baskets of clothes waiting to be folded.

But you know what? Once we started making time for sex, both of us started really looking forward to it again. The change in how we related to each other was immediate. It is much easier to hear that you need to pick up your socks from a woman who just made you feel amazing.

Laundry Day

Get out your calendar right now—seriously, right this minute—and schedule a sex date with your partner. If you have time to schedule a haircut, you have time to schedule sex.

KIM

I could be a spokesperson for Google Calendar. Everything changed for us after we started having sex again regularly. I cannot think of a moment in our relationship that was more of a turning point. We became kinder and more affectionate with each other and we cut each other more slack day-to-day. Scheduled sex has been the gift that keeps on giving. It's like food or exercise. If you eat junk food, you will crave junk food. But if you eat healthy foods, you'll crave healthy foods. If you are a slug, it's hard to get motivated to run. (Also, you have no legs, so . . .) But once you go for a few jogs, you start looking forward to that runner's high. That's how it was for us—sex begat more sex because we started craving it again.

THE ELEMENT OF SURPRISE

Now here is the curveball. We know we just told you that scheduling sex is our proven method for keeping our relationship intimate, but predictable consistency is the hallmark of sexless relationships, right? That's why we'd like to challenge you to set a goal of surprising your partner with sex totally out of the blue and/or totally out of your usual bedroom routine at least once in the next month.

There is a part of our relationship DNA that really needs to be surprised and delighted by unexpected awesomeness. Remember, novelty triggers dopamine, that feel-good chemical we all crave.

You have your warm, loving connection that you foster through regular, scheduled sex, but you also have space for your animal self who is unknown—and exciting. You want to be close enough to your partner that you feel trusting and connected, but independent enough that you are constantly discovering them. A break in routine fuels that excitement.

PENN

A few weeks ago, we were in the weeds (actually, it was more like we were in the Amazon jungle). Between the holidays and moving my dad out of his apartment and posting videos and troubleshooting Kim's HolderHamper and launching the wellness platform and, oh, yeah, being parents who also eat and sleep occasionally, we let the "laundry" pile up. Kim must have been as frustrated as I was, because one afternoon, she looked at me and asked, "Can we just go in the closet and do it?" I was like, "Yes, we can, and we will." The problem was, we had two people working in our living room at the time. But once Kim had said that, we were like a sleeper cell that had been activated. We had a mission, and we were going to execute. We made some flimsy excuse to our coworkers about needing to change a lightbulb or something and scrambled upstairs.

Once we closed the door, we giggled like teenagers and tried to be quiet, but then I realized that if we were too quiet, the people downstairs would be on to us, so as we were doing it, I started talking about mundane things: "You know what we should do later? We should go bowling."

Kim raised her eyebrows at me and asked, "What are you doing?"

I told her, "I'm putting the ruse on."

She gave me a giant smile and played along. Somehow, it was the hottest dirty talk. The fireworks were definitely popping. It wasn't a sexy firefighter scenario, but it was fantastic, and the best part was that we were really playful and fun with each other for days afterward.

JUST DO IT

Does all of this sound too good to be true? Could it really be the case that one five-minute conversation and a regular appointment for sex could have ripple effects throughout your marriage? We can't promise that it will change your lives. We can promise that it changed ours. The worst that could happen is that you have fun trying.

As a warning to our mothers, we will be talking more about how we really spiced things up in the bedroom in chapter 6. Feel free to skip that one if you gave birth to one of us.

06

I NEED TO SEE OTHER PEOPLE

THE FIGHT

PENN

This is not easy to write, but I need to see other people.

Here's the deal: when Kim needs to relieve stress, she shuts herself in our room with a magazine. Me? I am what psychologists call a "Flaming Extrovert." (It's in the *DSM*. Look it up.)

I have given a toast at every single birthday and wedding I've ever been to, even if I was the plus one. As Kim was delivering Penn Charles, I became best friends with the doctor—so much so that we were watching and commenting on a Panthers game as the baby was crowning. I'm on a first-name basis with the woman who takes delivery orders at our local Chinese place. I know the names of both of her children, what her all-time favorite movie is, and why she has her doubts about her daughter's new boyfriend (he uses *yummy* to describe things that aren't food). I get all my energy from other people—as many people as I can find and as often as I can find them.

The thing is, Kim and I do 95 percent of our work within the confines of our home, which means I interact with a very small number of people on any given day. There are weeks when I work my butt off but never leave my home. I take maybe a hundred steps a day. My Fitbit is very concerned about my cardiovascular health. As much as I adore my work and my wife, this extrovert needs outlets.

Enter tennis. Five years ago, I joined a local club and found there were hundreds of guys roughly my age who played for the exercise, the competition, and the Good Times. I loved it. After a couple hours of games, we'd head to the lounge where there was a TV, a bar, and plenty of conversation. It was love-love. (Tennis joke! Dad joke! Take your pick.)

But after a couple weeks of tennis nights with the guys, I could tell my wife was not as excited about this recurring social outing as I was. By the time I would be saying goodbye to my friends, my phone would be filled with text messages.

> Hope you're having fun! So I have both kids, one of them just scraped his knee. The other is having issues with her homework. What are we thinking is your ETA?

> PC is now crying because Lola took his basketball and threw it in the lake.

> Just making dinner plans. Are we coming home for dinner?

> Didn't hear from you. Guess we'll just see you when we see you. When is that going to be again?

This did *not* make me want to ask Kim for permission to go play tennis. So I regressed to a behavior I'd occasionally indulged in during my twenties. When we were living in New York and I needed a night out from our tiny apartment, I would shake my head pityingly and tell Kim I needed to get drinks with my good friend Will because he was going through a tough time. Poor guy. The truth was, Will was doing just fine; the meet-ups were my idea. I just wanted to go out and watch football and drink and laugh and talk about sports with strangers. When I'd come home smelling like booze, I would say, "Wow, Will is *really* sad. I'm glad I could help him work some stuff out."

I wasn't proud of this behavior, but hey, it got results. So when I got a hankering for a tennis match, instead of saying, "Hey, the guys are playing tennis and we're getting beers after; I'd like to go," I started saying something along the lines of, "Oh man, Vikram just canceled, and they're not gonna be able to play unless I show up. They're really counting on me. Ugh, I really want to stay home with you guys, but I feel like I need to be a saint and go. Okay? Okay. Bye!" Once again, I'd play the martyr in order to take time for myself.

But Kim is no dummy. After the third time I was called on to be the tennis hero, she looked and me and said, "Why don't you just bleeping say 'I want to go play tennis'?"

Why indeed.

KIM

I'm going to let you in on a little secret. I totally knew Penn was creating excuses to see his friends. Guess what? I didn't care. Not at first, anyway. It wasn't like he was off sleeping around or gambling away our savings. He was playing a sport, staying heart healthy.

How could I complain about that? Bless him; he even tried hard to get me to join, but it just did not click with me. Besides, when he went out, it meant I could indulge in an introvert's dearest wish: alone time.

You know how some people are adrenaline junkies who crave the thrill of leaping out of airplanes? I crave the thrill of slipping on my favorite pair of sweatpants. Don't get me wrong—I love people. I feel lucky to have a circle of friends who can make me laugh until I wet my pants (granted, it is not that hard: two kids > bladder control, amirite?), but I need my solitude. You know what else I need? Sleep. As time went on, Penn's tennis games increasingly left me with plenty of the former and zilch of the latter.

I go to bed early and I sleep lightly, so when games ran past nine o'clock or so (#earlybedtime4life), I would wake up when Penn came home. I swear there is something in a mother's brain chemistry that allows us to hear the handle on the screen door being depressed. One *click* and I am up for the rest of the night, and it fills me with irrational rage. What felt like no big deal at 6:00 p.m. began to feel like a Very Big Deal at 9:30 p.m. So after a while, when Penn would start hinting around that he wanted to go to a game, I was not having it with his dog and pony show. I wanted him to come right out and ask for it.

ASKING FOR IT

When Christopher heard about this dynamic, he dumped a cold bucket of reality on us by asking us to name a time when each of us had asked the other person directly for something we wanted. We looked at each other expectantly, like, "Go ahead, honey, you first." After a while, as we mentally cataloged all the ways we pussyfooted around expressing our needs, we realized he had us in a corner. We rarely, if ever, just came out and asked for what we wanted. Busted.

Christopher told us that avoiding asking for something you want is extremely common among couples, regardless of how long they've been together—and it is a hothouse for growing a healthy crop of marital resentment. Asking for what you want is vital if you are going to have a relationship in which both people can grow and stretch and not feel stifled and frustrated. That is why "Mature people ask for what they want" is one of Christopher's all-time favorite phrases. After he taught us how to do it, we started quoting it all the time. It has become an important part of our daily life, a mantra for marital satisfaction.

Before we Christophered this problem, a typical interaction for us went something like this: On his way to Chipotle, Penn would text Kim to find out what she wanted. She'd write back, "Get me whatever." Penn would order whatever he felt like. When he arrived home, Kim would look in the bag at the rice and beans he'd bought and say, "Why would you think I'd want beans?" The answer was because beans qualified as "whatever."

In matters trivial and important, we had gotten in the habit of dancing around our desires, dropping hints, and then crossing our fingers and hoping the other person would somehow intuit what we wanted, saying, "Behold! Here is a free pass for a weekend away with your friends," or "You know what? Why don't we stay home tonight and watch TV instead of going to that party?" We liked the idea that we shouldn't have to ask for what we wanted. After all, isn't that the whole point of being in it for the long haul? You put in the time so that the other person will get to know you well enough to anticipate your every desire. *La la la. Happily ever after. The End.*

Christopher convinced us that until we learn to ask for what we want or need, we're spinning our wheels, flinging mud behind us. We stay stuck in the same spot, digging deeper holes that fill up with grudges and bitterness. Before long, we're stranded.

Why do we repeatedly punk out?

REJECTED AND DEJECTED

According to Christopher, the first and most obvious obstacle to asking for what you want is a fear of rejection.

Sometimes, asking for what you want in an honest and straightforward way is all it takes. You ask, and—praise be—you receive. You say, "I'd like to rearrange our schedule for who drops the kids off at school because I have been late to work a lot lately," and *voilà*, you sit down and hammer out a new schedule.

However, asking is not a magic lamp you activate by saying, "I want." As Christopher says, we're all created in the image of God and given freedom of consciousness, will, and spirit, which means that it is possible that, for reasons of their own, your partner may not grant you what you desire. This can be difficult to accept. The prospect of being turned down can raise your blood pressure, not simply because you don't get what you want, but also because it's easy to misinterpret a no from your partner to mean "I don't care enough about you to say yes to that."

We experience a no as rejection, a smackdown sending us scuttling into our protective shells, rather than allowing for the possibility that there might be a perfectly good reason for our partner to refuse the request. One partner might say no to more date nights because they hate going to noisy restaurants where it's hard to have a real conversation, but the person asking hears "No more date nights" as "You don't want to spend time with me." Ouch.

Clever creatures that we are, we've learned that you can't be rejected if you don't ask. So after enough rejections, we stop asking. We don't ask for the attention we need, the change in the relationship, more time to ourselves, or whatever the need may be.

Revealing a desire, especially if it is a long-hidden one, is an act that requires massive vulnerability.

Hiding our desires is one of our most effective protection mechanisms because our needs are the most tender parts of ourselves. They lie close to our hearts, and some of them are so primal and raw it can be terrifying to share them with anyone—even the person who has watched you floss your teeth in your underwear.

Freud theorized that the id, the aspect of the psyche that houses our most basic desires for nourishment, affection, and survival, is the only part of us that has been around since birth, which makes it the longest-standing part of ourselves. Our needs and how well they are being fulfilled determine who we become. What we desire reflects who we are down at the core. We confuse the rejection of our requests with the rejection of our very selves. No wonder having your partner say no hurts as much as it does.

But the problem is that not asking at all leads to a stasis, enemy number one of intimacy. We implore you to make *mature people ask for what they want* your marriage mantra, too, if only because cultivating the vulnerability it takes to ask will lead to greater intimacy. No matter what happens, at the very least, you are moving closer together as a couple when one partner makes themselves vulnerable.

Making a request is like ice climbing: the only way to get moving is to take the risk of pulling the pick that's been holding you in place out of the ice, hold your breath, and then plunge it into the next spot so you can haul yourself up. To move forward, you must risk vulnerability.

Should I Ask for What I Want? (A Helpful Infographic)

We've designed this foolproof flowchart to help you determine whether your partner will grant you what you are asking for:

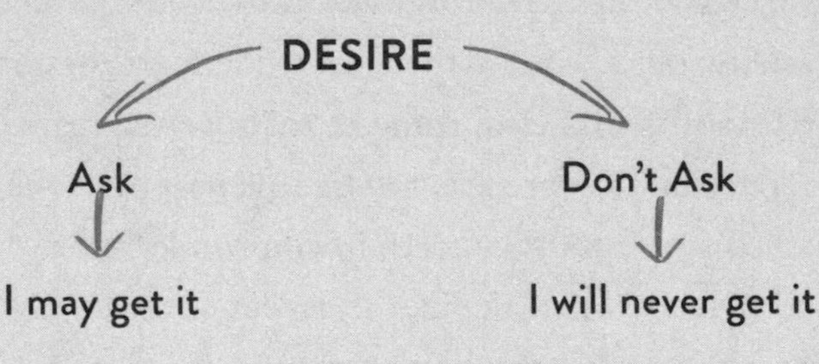

WHAT YOU WANT? BABY, I DON'T GOT IT; WHAT YOU NEED? BABY, I GOT IT

As we started to wrap our minds around how a fear of rejection was holding Penn back from getting his tennis time, Christopher helped us grasp that Kim was annoyed by Penn's tennis habit because she didn't understand it—and she didn't understand it because Penn didn't explain what his real need was. He didn't just *want* to play tennis. He *needed* to be around people. He was hiding the nature of his desire from her. When you are making an ask, there is an incredibly powerful and insanely simple way to increase your odds: just give a reason. We humans are suckers for the magic word *because*.

Back in the late seventies, Harvard professor of psychology Ellen Langer proved how powerful *because* can be. She set up an experiment in which the subjects had to ask someone who was in the middle of a big copying job if they could cut in and make copies of their own documents. The request was granted 60 percent of the time if the person didn't give a reason, but the success rate jumped to 93 percent if they did. We are not sharing this so that you can do Jedi mind tricks on your partner. We're sharing it because it says something about how important it is to say why you want what you want. *Because* can help you excavate the need beneath the want.

Let's look at why the difference between "want" and "need" is so crucial. A want is a concrete request; it is observable in the real world—a new iPod, better sex, more free time. But a need stems from that primal self, something to make you feel cared for and safe. Behind nearly every want is a need we're hoping to fulfill.

Here's something we like to do to drill down to find the need beneath our wants. We ask ourselves three "why" questions and then answer beginning with that magic word *because*.

For example:

Want: I want you to tuck in the dining room chairs after you get up from the table.
Why: Because I like a tidy house.
Why: Because it brings me peace.
Why: Because in a world where a lot of stuff is out of my control, having a clean house gives me a sense of control.

Want: I want you to eat less junk food.
Why: Because I'd like you to be healthier.
Why: Because I want you to live as long as possible.
Why: Because I don't want to end up alone.

Want: I want to spend part of our tax refund on a fancy watch.

Why: Because I'd like to own something I can wear my whole life.

Why: Because I want to pass it down to my child.

Why: Because I want him to remember me after I'm gone.

Three Whys, Man

Now you try. Next time you are about to ask for something from your partner, fill out the three whys to see if you can uncover the need beneath your want. Then during your conversation with your partner, make sure you give an explanation for what you are asking . . . just because.

I want ____________

Why? Because _______

Why? Because _______

Why? Because _______

PENN

Christopher helped me see that my mistake was not telling Kim why tennis was so important to me. I definitely had not done the three whys. Finally, Kim and I had the right "because" conversation. I told her, "Honey, I need this outlet. I love you. But I work in a job now where I'm in an editing bay for most of the day, and I don't really get enough human interaction. I need this part of my life because being social makes me feel sane, like I'm not alone in the universe." Of course she got it. Just because she is an introvert doesn't mean that she couldn't understand my need to get out of the house and connect with other people sometimes.

Having that conversation opened up something else for us too. I learned that my suspicions were right: my going out bothered her. But she didn't have FOMO (fear of missing out). She had FOMS—fear of missing sleep. A good night's sleep let her function better the next day. She was productive instead of spacey at work and kind instead of testy with me and the kids.

From that moment on, I agreed to sleep in the guest room on tennis nights.

Next time there was a tennis practice I wanted to go to, I caught myself saying, "Hey, so we're trying to get ready for a match that we have on Sunday, and if I don't go, we might not be ready for it . . ." I realized that I was doing it again. I was making excuses for why I needed to go out of the house. I heard Christopher's voice whispering in my head, "Mature people ask for what they want."

I stopped myself in the middle of the sentence and started over: "You know what, scratch that, I want to go play tennis tonight because I've been cooped up all day, and I need to see my buddies." It was one sentence, and bam, it was done. I don't know if it was because Kim had been primed by our Christopher lessons, but she just smiled, gave me a hug, and said, "Have fun." I think she meant it.

YOU ARE NOT A MIND READER

Going to the trouble to explain why you need what you want leads us to the second roadblock Christopher warned us about, which is the expectation that our partners, especially those we have known intimately for a long time, will be able to anticipate our desires without our saying a word about them. For the longest time, on Saturdays, Penn would take the kids to a coffee shop so Kim could have some peace at home, and when he'd come back, he would always bring Kim home a latte. So sweet, right? Yes, but . . . Kim doesn't really like lattes. But she hated to crush his generous heart. Why didn't she just tell Penn to bring her an Americano? This is a guy who felt comfortable burping in front of her six times a day, for crying out loud.

This went on for *years* (and that is a lot of steamed milk for someone who gets gassy when she has dairy). One day, Kim finally said, "Honey, you are an angel, and I don't deserve you, but I don't really enjoy lattes."

Penn was stunned. "But I've bought you the same drink for forever. You're just now telling me?" He wasn't mad, just confused. Didn't she trust him enough to ask for what she wanted? She had gotten into an awful habit of assuming he should know what she liked.

We are all guilty of this. We think, *If my partner really loved me, really knew me and what I care about, they would know what I want without my even having to ask*. Sounds dreamy, right? Like a total fantasy. Exactly. It *is* a fantasy. You are not telepathic, and neither is your partner. Try as you might, you cannot read someone's mind, and yet we've been conditioned to think that when we are under true love's spell, we are so in sync we are magically imbued with the ability to guess what the other person wants or needs—and when they don't, the disappointment is profound. We tell ourselves, *They must not value me enough to notice what I need*. Hogwash.

PENN

I like to think I have gotten to know Kim well enough over the years that I have a good idea what's going on inside her head and heart. I have definitely fallen for the myth that it is sexy when your partner intuitively knows exactly what you want and gives it to you, because it shows they are paying attention to you. But sometimes, no matter how observant I am or how well I think I know her, I miss something. One time, I missed something pretty big.

KIM

As we discussed, we went through a bit of a dry spell in the bedroom after our kids were born. We did manage to get back on track, and I was happy about that, and it really did turn our relationship around outside of the bedroom. But, if I am totally honest, I was not always feeling 100 percent fulfilled 100 percent of the time. While Penn and I had gotten back into a rhythm, let's just say most of the time not all of my needs were getting met. Did I mind? You know what? Yeah, I did, but I was really wrestling with my desire. Women have been taught that our sexual needs aren't important, and there were moments I thought maybe I should be satisfied because it just felt good to be next to my husband.

But after a while, resentment bubbled up. Something needed to change.

The idea of asking for something different between the sheets made my heart race, but I knew I had to do it. I had no idea how Penn would handle the I'm-not-getting-what-I-need talk. Would he take it personally? How could he not? As sexual beings, we are so fragile. I didn't want to crush his spirit or his mojo, but I couldn't continue with things the way they were.

I handled it like I do a lot of things—I put it on a calendar. I knew I wanted to have the talk at a time when I wouldn't be consumed with fifty other tasks, and I knew I wanted to have my clothes on during that conversation. So I asked him one morning, real casual-like, "Hey, I want to talk to you today—12:15, after lunch, whatever." Then I hightailed it to my office and buried myself in work.

By the time 12:15 rolled around, I had incredible pit sweat, the kind where it has already soaked under your armpits and is trickling down toward your elbow. It was weird to be nervous with this person who had seen my nether regions torn in two, but I bulldozed my way through it. I told him, "I want to make a change in our sex life. We've been getting in our sessions, but I'm not always getting what I need, and that doesn't work for me. It makes me feel like you don't care about my needs, which I know is not the case." I paused, took a deep breath, and said, "Okay, here's what I need. I want us to adopt a 'no partner left behind policy' in the bedroom because I am not enjoying this as much as I should. Nobody is leaving until we are both satisfied. If that means we're bringing in heavy artillery shipped to us in a weird brown box, then that's what we're doing." I braced for impact.

PENN

When Kim brought this up, my first thought was, "Oh crap. Do I suck at sex?" I did not reveal this outwardly, and I am glad I didn't, because forty-five seconds later when I looked up vibrators on the internet, I realized she wasn't getting a massive Penn replacement—she was getting this tiny thing that does something I can't do. When

I watched the demo video, I was like, "Man, I wish my penis could do that."

As I mentioned in the previous chapter, I enjoy sex, like, 1,000 percent more when we both are satisfied. If I know Kim's not super into it, it's not great. I think that is what differentiates humans from the rest of the animal kingdom. When you see animals doing it, oftentimes the lady animal is not having it. She's just looking off into the distance like, "Are you done? Can I get back to hunting now?" and the dude animal is all, "Just. One. More. Minute." But we humans care. Kim's arousal is a huge turn-on for me, so I was more than willing to do whatever it took to make sure she was satisfied.

There are still times when she gets there the old-fashioned way, too, which is awesome. I call it "beating the machine."

KIM

As soon as he said, "Game on. Let's do it. Let's go to AdamandEve .com, and let's pick out some toys," my muscles unclenched. I knew I'd made the right call.

Next thing I knew, he was running across the room to get his laptop, and he was like, "What about this one? What about this? Should we get two and try them out? How does that work? Oh, if you buy this, it comes with this free for me." He was all about the gift with purchase. He really leaned into it.

He needed to make me happy.

To be vulnerable enough to talk about our deepest needs was a huge step in our marriage. This one conversation changed a very important part of our relationship. Penn made it his priority to find ways to make me happy, and I did the very mature thing and told him exactly what I wanted. After that, little annoyances became less of a big deal to me. Don't get me wrong—I'm still annoyed that he can't find the hamper, but we had a new relationship after that. We really did.

Let me tell you, if you can have that conversation, you can have *any* conversation in a marriage.

How to Ask

Listening to Christopher when he said, "Mature people ask for what they want" has been a game changer for us. Here are some guidelines to make asking as painless as possible.

Put it in neutral. The temptation to hit your partner up for something when you feel like they owe you is strong. Instead of scorekeeping and waiting until your partner screws something up—like leaving the lights on or failing to hang up their coat for the ten thousandth time—ask in a moment of peace.

Steel yourself for seven seconds of suck. No matter how bad something is, you just need to get through the seven seconds of awkward. It rarely lasts much longer. Once you do the hardest thing, it gets better.

Eyes on the prize. Remember that your long-term goal is a close relationship with your spouse. Even if you don't get what you want, reframe your thinking about the conversation by focusing on the fact that you made your need known and your partner listened.

One thing at a time. No couple, no matter how much they love each other, can fix every single gripe in one conversation. It will always be an ongoing dialogue. Stick to one request at a time. Stay in that airport.

Be concrete, be specific. If you give a subtle ask, you will get a subtle response. Be as direct and specific as you can.

Use "because." Use the magic of a three-whys explanation to make sure that your partner understands what you need, not just what you want.

The long and the short of it is that no one will know what you want unless you tell them. Look your partner in the eyes and ask for what you want, because it just might change your marriage.

07

ARE YOU EVEN LISTENING TO ME?

THE FIGHT

PENN

We all blow it in the listening department sometimes, but not all "blowing it" is created equal. To help you figure out how badly you screwed up, I've taken the liberty of drawing up this handy list. You can think of it as the circles of hell in Dante's *Inferno*, only at the bottom, instead of watching Satan eat the heads off Judas and the guy who sold out Caesar, you're surrounded by husbands who were too busy looking at sports highlights to pay attention to their wives. Trust me when I tell you—that circle is *hell*.

- **Circle One**: When she tells you something from a room away and you can't hear her, but she keeps talking because she assumes you can hear every word and you don't bother to correct her.
- **Circle Two**: When she tells you three times to take the garbage out and you hear her, you really do, but you forget to do it.
- **Circle Three**: When she is talking about something serious, like her struggles with anxiety, and you space out while she's speaking and start thinking about how goats must feel about the goat yoga trend.
- **Circle Four**: When she is talking about how she is going to drink celery juice every day from now on and you think of something awesome that you want to say, but she has moved on to talking about how her mom might need surgery and you blurt out your celery thing from five minutes ago anyway.
- **Circle Five**: When you tune her out completely.

This is where this chapter's fight begins.

We were out to dinner with our friends Jake and Page. The conversation was lively, the wine was really good, and we were having such a fun time that I don't even remember what we ate, which is always the sign of a great evening. Because we are over thirty-five years old, we got to talking about our jobs. Kim and I often get questions about our work because 99.9 percent of people—including my parents—can't figure out how we make money. After Kim and I started working together full time, both of my folks kept offering me money because they assumed I was broke now that I wasn't on the news anymore.

The other thing that happens when we talk about how we make a living? People start bouncing around ideas for parody songs they think we should do. With apologies to the oncologist who suggested that we do a parody of Tina Turner's "Private Dancer" called "Bile Duct Cancer," some suggestions are . . . not great. But several ideas have been the sparks that got our videos going.

That night, Page said, "You know what? You guys should do a back-to-school video about Fortnite. Our kids will not stop playing it, and I don't know what's going to happen to them when school starts up again."

I pointed to her and screamed, "*Yes!* Every parent in America is freaking out about that." I could totally picture it. The lyrics were already scrolling through my brain. I turned to Kim and said, "I can't believe we haven't thought of doing that, honey!"

I looked at my honey.

She looked at me.

My honey was *pissed*.

She didn't say why. She simply looked at Page and said with a smile, "That is a great idea!"

I reached across the table and tried to hold Kim's hand, but she moved it away from me.

The deep freeze was *on*.

Fast-forward one hour later. On the way home Kim looked at me and said, "You do realize I told you earlier today, *to your face*, that we should do a back-to-school video on Fortnite?"

I most certainly did not realize that. Had she? Really?

Welcome to the Fifth Circle of listening hell.

I needed to know how I had ended up in that burning pit—and how to get out and stay out.

KIM

Not only had I suggested we make a parody video about the Fortnite craze *that very day*, I had even suggested songs to parody and lyrics that might work. At the time, Penn had nodded, but if you'd been watching our exchange, it would have looked to you like Penn was just humoring me because he wasn't really into the concept. That was my read on it. We would both be wrong. He wasn't humoring me. He was flat-out not listening. WTF.

When Page suggested the Fortnite parody, I had started to reply, "Yeah, that sounds like fun and our kids are the same way, but we thought of that already and decided against it," when Penn leaped up. It seemed that, magically, when someone else had the idea he could envision it perfectly.

I shouldn't have been surprised. This exact conversation has happened a thousand times before. I make a suggestion for a video we could make or a vacation we could go on or a new restaurant we could try, and Penn ignores it. But if that same video, vacation, or restaurant gets a mention from a friend? It's like he's hearing about the moon landing for the first time.

I knew going into this marriage that I was dealing with a chronic nonlistener. Early in our relationship you could almost see the steam coming out of Penn's brain as he made extreme efforts to focus on the words coming out of my mouth. But then a decade-plus later, you add in distracting kids, a dog, and a consuming job, and I can tell it's like he's perpetually fighting a band of monkeys banging cymbals in his brain. I get it, I do, but it doesn't change the fact that I want a partner who will f-ing listen to me.

I unleashed my normal, passive-aggressive self to get through the rest of that dinner. I did my closed-mouth smile. I forced a laugh. I'm sure it was completely obvious to our friends that I was not happy.

I was done being background noise while he listened to everyone else. Penn wasn't the only one who felt like he was in hell.

TWO EARS, ONE MOUTH

We Americans talk *a lot*. One study from the University of Arizona found that we spit out an average of over fifteen thousand words each day. True, about five thousand of those are a variation on "Has anybody seen my phone?" but it's an impressive output nonetheless. We pour an awful lot of effort into how we're going to say things. We prepare presentations, we rehearse our best stories to trot out at parties, and we replay conversations in our heads, writing our epic *8 Mile*–style comebacks, but we rarely spend a single moment preparing to listen. Big mistake. Listening is the most important thing you will ever do with your partner, and when you do it effectively, everything else in your relationship is just better. Christopher likes to remind us that there's a reason God gave us two ears but only one mouth.

We are social creatures, hardwired to crave connection. Our most potent way to connect is the exchange of tiny vibrations that travel through the air and put our ideas and experiences in someone else's head and vice versa. It's pretty incredible. When you think about it, even the most ordinary conversations about the weather or what you did over the weekend are small miracles. You're not thinking of a salad, a trout, or a rainstorm, and then someone says those words and suddenly you are. The fact that we can express complicated ideas about our experiences—about what it feels like to be your particular self in your particular body encountering a particular set of sensations and emotions as you engage with the world—is downright astonishing. When conversation flows, it can be transcendental. We all know the pleasure of a conversation where it's really humming along and every third sentence makes you want to grab your partner's arm and say, "OMG, *yes*!" There is such satisfaction when our words land deep in the gray matter of someone else's brain. Those moments of communing nourish us. We feel understood. We feel heard. We feel grounded.

By contrast, conversations where your words sail out into a vast canyon with no response make you feel lost in the wilderness with no way to triangulate your position in the world. It is insanely frustrating and deeply isolating to feel like people are not listening to you. It instantly turns you into *persona non grata*. Being ignored—or even half-listened to—is diminishing, dismissive, and downright lonely.

Listening is one of those skills we start to neglect the longer we are in a relationship. That was definitely what had happened for us as the years passed. We let our attention wander more often, even when the other person was reaching out.

After our Fortnite fail, Christopher helped us identify three of the biggest challenges to good listening habits: distractions, laziness, and interrupting. When one or both partners stop listening, communication dries up and your relationship is in danger of stagnation.

We read a great article in the *New York Times* by Kate Murphy, author of *You're Not Listening*, about modern listening habits. Friends, the news is not good. Murphy cited a study that showed most people were more likely to talk about something personal with someone they barely knew than they were to spill their guts to their closest people. We like to think of this as the airplane habit—you know, when you confess your deepest, darkest secrets to the person who happens to be sharing your armrest. What's up with that? Why should we gift our intimate thoughts, fears, and hopes to someone who is going to forget about us before they even reach the baggage carousel? Something has gone majorly awry.

So what's to be done? Let's start by examining the most common bad listening habits.

PENN

Because of my ADHD, for a long time I assumed I was just a bad listener. But after talking to Christopher, I realized that I can't escape the responsibility to listen, especially to Kim, just because it doesn't come easily to me. This is my marriage. And my life. Being able to listen carefully is a craft and a tool. You can get better at it. Strike that. You *must* get better at it. Being able to listen carefully is an essential skill. It's not like you have to learn how to figure skate and someone is going to hold your kid hostage unless you land a triple toe loop. But this matters big-time. So listen up.

DRIVEN TO DISTRACTION

In chapter 5, we talked about the way activities pile up and draw us away from our relationship. Those distractions keep us from making the time to connect to each other. Here, we want to look at how you can be distracted even when you set aside the time to connect. You can be too distracted to talk to your partner when you are in the same room—or even in the same bed. How many conversations have you had with your partner that included the following?

- "Just a second, I need to . . ."
- "Sorry, I was just texting. What did you say?"
- "I missed what you just said."
- "Were you talking to me?"
- "What was that?"

We live in a world in which it's so easy to be distracted. There are dings and rings everywhere you go. Not that long ago, people amused themselves in the evenings by sitting around and listening to someone play the fiddle by the light of a lantern. Okay, yes, we got that image from *Little House on the Prairie*, but we're pretty sure it's accurate. But now, we scroll through our phones in the evenings while watching Netflix with a Spotify playlist on in the background. There are so many things demanding our attention.

Christopher constantly reminds us that if we are going to have any hope of actually connecting with each other, we need to go off the information grid every once in a while. Shut off our devices. Close our calendars; put work on pause. Date night's not the night to return emails. A person is not going to feel heard if you keep saying, "Let me finish this text and then we'll talk."

In our house—and we'd wager the same holds true for you—the phone is the biggest culprit. If you are going to take one piece of advice in this chapter, make it this: part of each day, put the dang phone away. Put it out of sight. Get it out of there. Put it in one of those phone jails where you have to smash the glass with a hammer to get at it, and then throw away the hammer. Smart phones were deliberately engineered to keep us coming back to them over and over again, even when there is something and someone objectively more important to pay attention to breathing the same air as you. It is really freaking hard to conquer the addiction and really hard to listen when you are competing with a device specifically designed to suck up all your attention. We have learned that we cannot talk to each other if one or both of us has a cell phone on our persons. When we need to have a serious discussion, we'll send the kids up to their rooms or out in the yard and we go to a deserted island together. And by island we mean a couch, a bed, a bench, a chair. Anything to get us off the floor, truly alone together, with no distractions. TV is off, phone is away, and we're looking at each other. We're listening.

3–2–1 Contact

The simplest way to show courtesy to somebody is to look them in the eyes. Notice we said simplest, not easiest. It is actually weirdly hard to look at your partner for more than a few seconds. But boy, will they feel like you're listening to them when you do.

Each day, try for five uninterrupted minutes where you focus exclusively on each other—and make two of those full contact. Eye contact. Sit down, and as you're talking, make eye contact with your partner.

It's so awkward that we advise the step-up method. Start slow, with just thirty seconds, then add another thirty seconds each day until you can look at each other for two minutes while you have a five-minute conversation.

PENN

We recently took the deserted island concept to the next level.

Kim and I took a vacation where we spent two weeks without internet. That's right—we went fourteen days without phones. Or a computer. Or even a graphics calculator. Kim was nervous to be gone that long and without constant contact with the kids. For my part, at first, I felt like I had lost a limb. I had a phantom appendage that was refusing to give me sports scores. But very quickly, something amazing happened. Without my phone to distract me, I could give Kim the full bore of my attention. (I did not mean that to sound gross, but it really does, doesn't it?) I was so tuned in to her moods that I started being able to anticipate when she was about to have a panic or anxiety reaction. It was like I had become a highly trained helper dog with better hair.

One afternoon, we were going on a side trip that required a quick plane flight. To prepare, Kim packed her overnight backpack forty times before we left. It was a work of art. I, on the other hand, put all my stuff on the bed and then lifted the comforter to slide everything into my bag like a dump truck. Done and done. At check-in, security made Kim empty everything in her Jenga bag onto the floor, and then they wouldn't let her pack it back up correctly. They yelled over her shoulder, wanting her to make room for the next group. She did as they asked—she wasn't trying to get pulled out of line and taken to an undisclosed location for questioning—but she was definitely wobbly as she did it.

Now, if I had had my phone with me, these events might have registered, but then I would have clicked on a video of some guy who can hit a Frisbee with a Ping-Pong ball from two hundred yards away and I would have gone mentally AWOL. But I didn't. Instead, I tuned in to the fact that even though it looked on the surface like Kim was keeping it together, we were at threat level 1,000.

When we reached our room, she flooded. I could tell she was going through it and a panic attack was nigh.

Over the years, I have learned that when Kim is having a panic attack, she doesn't want me to hug her tightly or do anything drastic. She would prefer, say, a hand gently placed on her hand. I got her a glass of water. I found her a blanket. I got her a Kleenex. It's amazing how many things you can pick up on if you're focusing on your partner 100 percent.

I just listened to her. I didn't try to fix anything. I just said, "This really sucks," and it was like magic. We felt close to each other, really close to each other.

That night, she took a piece of the hotel stationery and hunched over it for a second. She drew a fake award that said BEST HUSBAND EVER and put it on my bedside table. You know what? In those moments I felt like it.

PARDON THE INTERRUPTION

Sometimes, we don't listen because we are too busy speaking. There are times when figuring out who gets to speak becomes a power struggle. As Christopher has told us, after money and sex, power is the subject couples struggle with most often. When you are talking over each other, you're battling over who gets to determine the conversation in your relationship.

We had Dan Sipp, an instructor who uses improv techniques to show people how to communicate better, on our podcast to talk about how our conversations can feel like power struggles. The first thing he talked to us about was interruptions. Interrupting a fellow improv performer is the equivalent of a technical foul in basketball or roughing the passer in football. It's terrible form and you should avoid it at all costs. Dan told us that there are two different kinds of interruptions: (1) butting in when someone is talking, which is the kind of interruption we're most familiar with, and (2) non-kinetic interruption, when you have something you are so excited to share, you stop listening to what other people are saying while you wait for your chance to say your piece. Even though you haven't *technically* interrupted, you have disconnected from the conversation. You're like a little kid who really, really wants to show off the worm they found in the yard, regardless of what the adults are talking about. You're not listening to a word they're saying. All you can think about is the thought wriggling in your brain.

PENN

The first line of my bio should be "Penn Holderness is from a gigantic family in the South." I love a big, crowded dinner where everyone is talking at once as much as Kim hates them. When I get bored, I can just swivel my head around and no one thinks I'm being rude. I love being able to bounce from one conversation to the next. But when there are a lot of people talking, it's tough for me to hold my tongue—I feel like I have to let my thoughts out because my mental bladder is full.

During a conversation, when I hear something interesting, my brain goes, *Oh, here's one way to respond to that. Hey! This is really creative. I can say this, this, this, this, this, and* this! *Oh man, this is going to be good. Wait till they hear. Ugh. Is that guy still talking? I better get it out before it's too late.* Then I say whatever I had cooking. Hold for laughter. I now recognize that this is non-kinetic interruption. I'm so good at it that even when Dan Sipp was on our show discussing how to not interrupt, I was thinking about my next comment while he was talking! I realized I do this all the time, and no one is immune to it, not even the most scintillating conversationalists . . . not even Kim.

One time, we were at a barbeque with some friends, and someone commented on her earrings. I don't wear earrings, so I started thinking about my outfit, and how I thought I was showing too much chest hair with the shirt I was wearing, but if I buttoned it up another button I would look like a dork. Right then and there my brain was like, *Holy crap, I have a solution for this!* So I blurted out, "Do you ever wonder why they don't have an extra button in between these two buttons? Could we invent a shirt that has a tweener button?" (I still think this is a freaking great idea. If someone figured it out they could make a bunch of money on it. If not, dibs!)

Our guests smiled and acknowledged that it was not a bad idea. I took a swig of my beer, feeling pretty proud of myself.

Kim was not proud.

She held her tongue through dinner, but on the way home she said, "Hey, that was really rude when you interrupted me tonight."

"When?" I asked. She explained that it was when I pitched my In Buttween (working title). I started to apologize for interrupting her during her story about . . . but then I realized I had no idea what she had been talking about when I got all excited about my shirt thing. None.

She told me that the earrings she was talking about were made by abused women in Africa and were being sold by a very cool local woman who wanted to support developing-world fashion. Kim had been in the middle of telling some very powerful stories about the lives this woman has changed when I went all in on the Stud Button. (Better name? I'll do a Google poll.)

Back then I was confused about why she was so upset. In my head, I was like, *But did you not hear what I said? It was such a great idea!* Besides, I thought, conversations are supposed to jump around. Now I feel embarrassed when I tell the story about the Butt-in (patent pending).

KIM

To be fair to Penn, I know that his brain is a snake pit of non-kinetic interruptions waiting to strike. It's his ADHD. In the beginning, I just thought that Penn's ADHD meant "Oh, he's high energy. Fun!"

Isn't that cute? The blinders you put on when you're dating. There are so many positives that come with Penn's ADHD. For one thing, it fuels his extreme creativity. Plus it gives him a very low tolerance for things that are boring, which is useful when you produce stuff for people to watch on the internet. His thing is, "If I get bored editing something, I know nobody will watch it." And that's working for us.

So, yes, in many ways, his ADHD is a gift, but it can be trying.

He loses his inhaler so often that we've run out of insurance money to cover it and we have to pay cash for new ones. I have bought him AirPods as gifts three times this year alone. A few weeks ago, he texted me, "Hey, just letting you know I took a big tablespoon of peanut butter to have a peanut butter lollipop as a snack. I didn't have any of it, and now I can't find it. I love you, bye."

We have yet to find that spoon.

For the most part, I feel for the guy, and I try to roll with it. But I have the hardest time adapting to living with a partner who has ADHD when I can tell he's just not listening. I will tell him a story about how I nearly twisted my ankle during a run, and then ten minutes later he'll ask me, "Do you think you're going to go for a run today?" Okay, yeah, my story might not have been a scene out of *War and Peace* or even *Peanuts*, but it was *my* story, and I expected him to listen. I know it's not true, but sometimes it feels like he's twisting his mustache and saying, "I don't have to listen because I have ADHD. *Hahahaha*." It cuts deep when I don't feel heard because I really love the guy. I value his opinion. I want us to experience things together, and I want to talk about them with him after they happen. It hurts when I feel like I can't hold his attention.

GOOD LISTENING GEOMETRY

We are all guilty of hijacking a conversation now and then, even if we are not explicitly interrupting. We suffer from what we call "So did I!" syndrome. One partner will say, "I had a terrible day of work," and the other partner might respond, "So did I!" and then go into details about how horrible his day was instead of giving her the space to unload about hers. At first glance, this might seem like a point of connection, of commonality, but we are willing to bet that the first person talking does not feel that way. She probably feels like her partner is a self-centered jerk who didn't let her say her piece. At best, he has half listened as he began a parallel conversation. As you'll remember from geometry, parallel lines never meet. That is no way to feel connected. It's a natural thing to want to share your experience to make a connection, but it is not the right way to connect. You have to intersect with your partner when you talk. You need to learn how to use the magic words *yes, and*.

YES, AND

"Yes, and" is a foundational part of improv comedy, and it should be a foundational part of the way you talk to your partner. When actors get up in front of an audience to improvise a scene, there's no script, no direction—just the faith that they are going to make it work together. Because they are starting from scratch, every line they speak needs to build on what has come before; otherwise, the scene quickly devolves into what amounts to nonsense or petty squabbling. For instance, imagine a scene in which an actor begins the action by pretending to pull another actor over for speeding, saying, "I'll need to see your license and registration, please." If the other actor says, "No, but you're a cowboy!" the scene screeches to a halt and becomes an argument about facts—is the person a police officer or a cowboy? When that happens, you're in "Who is right?" territory instead of "How can we go forward together?" territory. Now imagine the second actor had run with the speeding suggestion, saying, "Yes, officer, and I'm sorry, I didn't realize my horse could do eighty." They've accepted the initial premise and added their two cents but still moved the scene forward.

KIM

One of the best things we learned from Christopher about how to be a better listener is how to look for ways to build on what your partner is saying using the "yes, and" technique. "Yes, and," he told us, is the mirror image of "no, but." "Yes, and" is useful when you are enjoying a peaceful, loving conversation, but it changes everything during a disagreement. When I feel myself getting defensive in an argument, I remind myself to "yes, and." I listen to what Penn is saying and then try to build on it instead of tearing down whatever he has said. Penn will say, "Let's do a video where we spill beer all over the kitchen floor." Instead of nixing the whole idea because I do not want my kitchen smelling like a bar, I'll say, "Yes, good idea, and we can do it with Coke." He feels heard, and I feel happy.

I'M NOT BIASED; *YOU'RE* BIASED

The next habit to attack is thinking you're smarter than you are. We don't care if you are a genius who understands how Bitcoin works (wait, but if you are, can you please DM a quick explanation, or maybe just shoot us a cryptocurrency investing tip?)—regardless of how bright you are, you are not a fortune teller. You cannot predict what your partner is going to say every time they open their mouth to speak.

Getting to know what makes your partner tick is one of the great joys of life. Learning about someone else's inner world—their hopes, joys, fears, quirks, weaknesses—makes our own inner worlds that much bigger. As we get to know someone, we gather so much data, picking up on patterns of how our partners think, what their concerns are, and how they speak about them. We learn to anticipate when they are going to make a pun or say "Amirite?" or yell "Psyche!" It is satisfying and comforting, like learning the words to your favorite song. But your partner is not a song on repeat. Their tune is improvised as they grow, change, morph, develop, and evolve, which means they are inherently unpredictable. When we go into auto-complete mode with our partners, rushing to fill in the blanks before they've even had a chance to get all of their words out, we are not being fair to them.

In Kate Murphy's *New York Times* article, she pointed out that people are especially bad at paying attention to their partners. We do way better at understanding strangers. Our novelty sensors perk up and we attune to information better when it comes from someone new rather than our trusty old spouses. Dudes. Come on! In psychology, this is referred to as the *closeness communication bias*. Our Fortnite fight was a blazing example. Penn had listened to Page more carefully than he had to Kim.

KIM

That wasn't the first time Penn showed closeness communication bias, nor will it be the last. In fact, we were recently interviewed by the *New York Post*. I told the reporter about how I'd spent hours and hours making silly videos all by myself with a clunky camcorder long before there was any way to share them with an audience beyond my very patient parents.

Penn looked at me like I had just told him my real name was Gertrude. "You did? You're telling me that you're basically doing the same thing you were doing when you were thirteen years old except now people watch you?" It was awkward.

"Yes, honey," I said, "I must have told you that a million times."

He had no idea. I'm willing to bet that the same scenario plays out in kitchens and dining rooms and bedrooms all over the nation.

It's not entirely our fault as listeners. It's a two-way street. When we know someone well, we get conversationally lazy. We think, *Of course they know what I'm saying. Weren't they there last time this happened?* We use shorthand, we don't give enough details or context for our stories, and we say far less to help our partner understand what we mean than we would to a stranger, a habit that can become dangerous over time. After enough communication misfires, what's the point of even trying to talk to your partner?

ONE PLUS ONE IS ONE

We think we have a pretty good answer to that. Your partner makes your story more interesting. As crucial as it is to listen to what your partner says day-to-day, it is even more important to listen to the intricate story your partner is telling you over time, the story of their life. One of the essential roles—maybe the *most* essential role—we play for our partners is as audience to their life stories. That is the core promise we make when we enter into the covenant of a long-term relationship: *I will witness your story, I will listen as you grow and change and stretch. I will be a sensitive receptacle to your most precious narrative, the story of your life. I will care how it turns out.*

If you don't attend to the ways your partner is constantly growing, blossoming, wilting, and then sprouting new buds, your communication is going to be pretty barren.

Now, most of us don't go around oral tradition–style narrating the story of our lives. But we do report small moments during our days—the frustrations, the tiny surprising joys, the jokes—all the stuff we are taking in, the stuff that affects us and makes us who we are. We want you to listen to that stuff. Be like a sponge that becomes less brittle the more it absorbs.

Over time, as we pay close attention to each other, our individual stories become beautifully entwined. Christopher calls this the *calculus of marriage*, where, magically, one plus one equals one. He shared a moving poem with us by Wendell Berry. It's called "The Blue Robe," and it's told from the perspective of someone in a long and loving relationship. The narrator describes the quiet joy of sitting together with his beloved late in life, knowing more about each other now than they did when they first met. He describes how his heart quakes to see her now a grandmother in a blue robe. Berry writes that they no longer have two separate stories, but "we belong to one story / that the two, joining, made . . ."

How good is that? "We belong to one story / that the two, joining, made"! You're writing your story together. That's marriage.

PENN

At the risk of sounding cheesy, I have to say that that is exactly how it has played out for us, and learning to listen to each other has been the force that joined our two stories into one. I can't remember the last time I had a conversation with someone and didn't bring up Kim in the first two sentences. We are inextricably part of each other's lives. That's what I love about "The Blue Robe." The poem captures the idea that our two stories have become one and are the better for it.

For us, the blue robe is a beach somewhere. It's the mentality of an oasis where the two of us can throw away our phones because we have so much where we are that we don't need them anymore. It's a metaphor for a place where we can be together the way we were in that hotel room on vacation, connected, in tune with each other, and building something beautiful together.

Plus margaritas.

ACTIVE LISTENING

While we think you should listen to your partner all the time, there are some conversations that require extra care and attention. These are usually the talks that have the potential to turn into fights—when you disagree or feel hurt or want to make a change. We want you to get those right, so we asked Christopher to come up with some good listening guidelines for important conversations.

He started by reminding us that listening is not a passive activity. While you don't even have to move to do it, it still takes work, and like many things that require work, when it comes to listening we humans are total slackers. If you want your marriage to thrive, you need to switch gears from passive listening to active listening.

You might be familiar with active listening, but here's a quick refresher.

When you are listening, you actively check in with your partner to make sure that what you are hearing is what they are saying. Try to think of your conversations as building something together. Your conversations should be like bricklaying. You can't just have two stacks of bricks next to each other. They'll collapse. You need to interlock and overlap in order to build something lasting. Collaboration is your conversation cornerstone.

As Christopher told us, if you're not good at piano, you practice and you get better. Same deal with listening. If you're not good at it, you practice and you get better. Try these techniques next time you need to have a significant conversation with your partner:

I'm all yours. Right off the bat, set a clear intention to be there for your partner. Jettison those distractions and say aloud that you are there to listen. Just knowing that you are there and have dedicated time to listen is a huge step.

Magic words:

"What's on your mind?"
"I'm all yours."
"I want to hear what you have to say."

Hold the help. True listening means hearing the person so completely that you can put yourself in their shoes and understand what they're going through. It's not about taking that data and fixing it. Don't parachute in and try to solve the problem. You're not a smoke jumper.

Magic words:

"Tell me more."
"Can you clarify that for me?"

Repeat. Repeat. As goofy as it sounds, it's very effective to use your own words to repeat what you've heard your partner say. It shows that you are taking to heart and processing the information they've given you.

Magic words:

"Here's what I heard you say. Did I get it right?"
"Let me make sure I'm understanding."
"You said [repeat word or phrase], and you meant . . ."

But don't ask for anything. When your partner asks you to sit down with them, it's not an invitation to list your own grievances. You can't listen if you are doing all the talking.

Magic words:

Silence. Because you're listening.

Perform a postmortem. Then, at the end of the conversation if it's an important one, do a little recap, just to underscore that you understood the main points your person was trying to convey.

Magic words:

"In essence, what you wanted me to know was . . ."

"So we've agreed . . ."

Is Your Partner Ready? Or REDdy?

There are definitely times when the listener is at fault for not paying attention. But the person talking has to shoulder some of the responsibility too. A huge part of this is choosing your moment. It's hard to listen when a firehose of demands is hitting you in the face. Bath time is probably not the time to work out a longstanding issue with your schedules. Neither is at the end of a tiring day where your partner has just been in back-to-back meetings. But maybe a long car ride is. Or a weekend coffee break. You need to set the stage for success. It comes down to timing and mutual readiness.

Dan Sipp made one of our favorite suggestions about improving listening. He told us about an improv game called the red ball exercise. Players take turns pretending to pass an imaginary red ball to one another. The catch is that they have to make eye contact and say "red ball" before they are allowed to "throw" it to someone. Once that person confirms their readiness by saying "Okay, red ball" in response, the ball can be thrown.

You can use this as shorthand to ask your partner if they are ready to listen. It's important to remember that the answer can be no—and if that's the case, don't throw that ball. Kim used to be terrible at this. Penn would come in from carpool and before he even set his keys down, she would launch a red ball at his face. Don't do that.

You might have to hold that ball until later in the day when your partner is ready to say, "Okay, red ball."

08

YOU DON'T TAKE ME SERIOUSLY

THE FIGHT

KIM

You know how people talk about going to their happy places? Usually, they fantasize about relaxing on a white sand beach in Negril or enjoying the view from the top of the Swiss Alps. Me? My happy place is thinking about the future. When I have a quiet moment, that's where my mind goes for kicks. *Where will we be in five years? I wonder what we're going to be doing. Are we going to be making videos for a machine that hasn't even been invented yet? Will I understand TikTok?* I love to play those games because you never know what life is going to hold for you. Five years ago, Penn was a news anchor and I was just starting a production company. Now look at us.

But futurecasting is not Penn's favorite thing to do. Earlier this year, we were driving back from a dinner out with the kids. It had been a goofy, fun, no-phones-in-front-of-us family meal. Everybody was in a great mood, so I let my mind wander over to my happy place. When I get into that mode, every single sentence starts with "What if . . ." That day, I had a big "What if"—one that I'd been chewing on for a while. I thought to myself, *What if we could write a musical?* I knew it was far-fetched. Yes, we make song and dance numbers for a living, but our videos are for people to stare at for a few minutes on a device in the palm of their hand for free. This would be a *production*—IRL, with full-sized humans. This would be something with an intermission and seats that people would have to pay for. We would have to invest a lot of time and money, and I had no idea where to start. Stage shows are famously hard to produce; more often than not, they fail. But I love live theater so much, and hey, we *do* write song and dance numbers for a living.

I was nervous even to talk to Penn about this dream because it was so out there. But I'd had a really nice relaxing dinner with my family—and maybe a glass of wine—so before I could chicken out, I said to Penn, "I've always dreamed of writing a live show, and I think you and I could do it. I could write the story; you could write the songs. What if it went to Broadway? What if I start crafting that?"

Zero seconds later, Penn replied, "Do you think that's the best use of your time?"

Just like that, it was *adios, happy place*. It felt like I had been punched in the chest. I was stunned. It's not like I said, "Let's start a car dealership . . . on the moon!" This was, if not in our actual wheelhouse, at least wheelhouse adjacent. I'd actually thought it was a pretty good idea.

I didn't want to scream in front of the kids, so points for me for not shouting, but I am not proud of what happened next. I asked (asked/demanded, potato/potahto) Penn to stop the car, and then before it even rolled to a stop, I got out and walked the rest of the way home. I knew Penn was driving beside me trying to get me to get back in the car, but there was no way I was riding shotgun with a dream killer, so I just kept walking. When I got home he was waiting in the driveway, but I walked past him as if I didn't even see him. He followed me inside, genuinely confused about what he had done wrong. He had no clue why I was so hurt.

He fumbled for the right words, but none came. I started crying, and immediately he started firing off apologies like an Uzi releasing "I'm sorrys."

PENN

Kim described that situation perfectly. I have no edits or revisions. That is exactly what happened. I was sorry. I just didn't know for what.

She gives me grief for not liking the what-will-we-be-doing-in-five-years game, but I have big dreams too. Like sometimes when I am about to go to sleep, I imagine myself playing small forward for UNC, or playing piano for Freddie Mercury, or starring on SNL.

I want you to understand that what went through my head when Kim pitched her idea and what came out of my mouth were two different things. In my head, I was like, *A musical, huh? Hmmm. We already have so much going on with our business and our family. Do we have time for this? You know what, Kim is working so hard, if we're going to produce a musical, I feel like that is something we should let other people help us with.* That's what was going through my head. My brain was like, *Penn, you're awesome at this.*

You know those scenes in Bugs Bunny cartoons where they show you what goes on inside a machine? With all those gears, and a mallet, and a hamster powering it? When I opened my mouth, one of those contraptions inside my head transformed my supportive statement from "You're a great wife with too much on your plate already" into "Is that really the best use of your time?"

Usually, when something is coming out of my mouth, and I have the thought, *Huh, should I have said that?* the answer is NO. If there's even the smallest question, there is a 100 percent chance I just screwed up. I'll be honest: in this situation, I didn't have that feeling. I actually had this feeling of pride and restraint because what I wanted to say was, "Are you bleeping kidding me?"

And the next thing I knew, Kim was not in the car anymore.

She just got out and walked her angry walk. When Kim angry walks, there is no mistaking it. Those are the special footsteps that say "I am using my feet to walk like this so I do not use my fist to punch like this." She can clear a room in four steps, so she got home fast. Also, we were only like a hundred feet away. Seriously, you could already see our lawn when she opened her car door. It took me about six seconds to pass her and beat her home.

I do appreciate her not punching me. But I *do not* appreciate the silent treatment. It is torture for me. When the most important person in my life seemingly hates me, I will cave every time and do whatever is needed for sound to come back. I will apologize as profusely as possible to make the tension go away.

So that's what I did. I explained to her that I simply didn't want her to burn out, that I cared for her and supported everything she does. It still took her a while to cool off, but eventually we went back to normal.

So there you have it. She felt something. I felt something. She said something. I said something. She got out of the car and walked home. I caved and said I was wrong.

By the way, I still don't think I was wrong.

Was I wrong?

ATTACHMENT THEORY

As you might suspect, this was not just a case of who was right and who was wrong. Christopher pointed out that sure, it may be true that we are far too busy to cram another massive project into our schedule, so Penn might not have been wrong about that, but whether we were destined to be the next Rodgers and Hammerstein was hardly the point. So what was? Why did a simple question send Kim flying out of the car? And why did her silent treatment turn Penn into an I'm-sorry machine?

As we were talking to Christopher about this fight, we noticed the word *alone* kept popping up. What was going on there? Sure, no one likes to feel alone, but why had both of us freaked out like our mothers had just forgotten us at the mall? Actually, that's pretty much what was going on in our brains.

Maybe you've heard of *attachment theory*. You probably learned about how it describes the bond between parent and child. A child can be securely attached, insecurely attached, or avoidant, depending on how reliably their parents take care of their needs. Securely attached is the good one, in case that isn't clear. It turns out, in recent years psychologists have determined that a similar dynamic is at play in adult romantic relationships. There are books and books on the subject, and we highly recommend that you look into them (a particularly good one is Rachel Heller and Amir Levine's *Attached*), but since we're not psychologists, we'll boil it down to the basics. Attachment theory says that the bonds we form with our partners are very similar to the ones we have with our parents—we depend on them for support and caretaking. If we are going to feel securely attached to our partners, we expect them to be *nearby, accessible,* and *attentive.* When we get all of that from our partners, we are happy campers who can enjoy life and each other, and we're able to handle the occasional bump in the road.

Couples with secure attachment

- stay attuned to each other's needs
- live in the now
- offer intimacy
- feel like they have control over their own lives
- fully accept and feel fully accepted by each other
- seek support when necessary
- express emotion fluently
- face difficulty head-on

When you feel protected and safe in your connection with your partner, you can go about your life with the confidence that comes from knowing you are happily attached—just like a toddler can play happily if he isn't constantly having to look over his shoulder to make sure his mom is in the room. Your partner is like base camp when you're out there exploring the universe in a space suit. If you're communicating well and feeling securely attached, it's like you're tethered to your partner by one of those hoses that connect astronauts to the space station so they aren't lost in space. You know that you can return to a place where you can breathe easily after exploring the vast solar system. But when that connection is under threat—whether it's a distracting new someone, a communication misfire, a lack of appreciation—in scientific terms, we freak out. Have you ever heard a baby screech the screech of death when its mother leaves the room? That's what our souls feel like when we don't feel secure in our attachments, like we've been cut free and left to float aimlessly in a cold, dark place.

So what do we do? Like big babies, we engage in what psychologists refer to as *protest behaviors* to get our partners to attend to our needs. We'd like to help you look at your behavior when you fight and figure out if you are acting out because you feel like your attachment is not secure. Then we'll share three little magic words that will go a long way toward repairing a frayed bond. They're not what you think.

WE DOTH PROTEST TOO MUCH

Since we are not actually big babies—at least most of the time—our protests look a little more sophisticated than tossing your cereal on the floor or pitching a fit in the grocery store, but they are equally expertly designed to get your partner to pay attention to you.

Here are a few common ways adults act out when they don't feel a secure sense of attachment to their partners:

- Texting, calling, and then texting and calling again. *Just saying hi. Where are you? What are you doing? Where have you gone? Why have you abandoned me?*

- Playing chicken. You won't reach out to fix matters until they do.
- Withholding warmth. No sexy time, no hugging, no smiles, no nothin'.
- Running away from conflict. (Ahem, Kim.)
- Ignoring. Avoiding your partner or doing that thing where you are in the same room but *definitely not* paying attention to them.
- Shutting down. Clamming up or giving in without a real discussion.
- Being downright mean. Name-calling, snide comments.
- Pushing buttons. Playing to your partner's insecurities.
- Inducing jealousy. Mentioning another person repeatedly, texting secretively.
- Saying whatever it takes to make things right. Apologizing, buying gifts—anything but actually addressing what made you feel unsafe. (Ahem, Penn.)

Christopher reminds us all the time that the longer you're with your partner, the better you are at loving them, because over time you learn how to love them better. If you use those powers for good, then you can enjoy the calm that comes from a secure attachment. But guess what else you get better at with time? You learn how to get under your partner's skin with just one word or one look or one action. You know which protest behavior will get their attention the fastest. Maybe you call your wife by your mother's name. Maybe you remind your husband of a time he forgot to pay the mortgage. Maybe you make a comment under your breath about how it wouldn't hurt if your partner went to the gym once in a while.

PENN

Or maybe you say something that makes your partner think you are always hoping something better will come along. I know Kim's favorite pastime is to play future funtime, and at some level, I get it. Like I said, I have dreams too. But the dreams that I have are super far-fetched, like I'll just sit and imagine myself as Batman. Kim's constant dream-chasing can feel relentless.

That day in the car, we were at a place in our lives where I was already getting a little frustrated by the volume of dreams. She was several months and thousands of dollars into development on a travel product. She had just begun conversations about an online wellness course. She wanted to hire two more people to work for us full time to expand our ability to create content. Let me be clear: none of this was taking away from her contributions with our day-to-day—she was just waking up earlier and staying up later and working nonstop to get all of this done—but the idea of adding something else when we already had so many things was too much. My tendency is to focus on what is already working, and then after those projects have reached their conclusion, maybe try a new thing.

If I'm honest with myself, I can admit that dream-chasing and futurecasting bother me for another reason too: I like where we are now. We have it really, really good. We've got jobs we love, kids who can wipe their own butts, and a dog who is so adorable that I am more than happy to pick up her poop. I could just sit and survey my kingdom happily until the end of time. If we are in exactly the same place five years from now, I will be *psyched*. My feeling is if we don't spend some time appreciating our hard work and how far we've come as a family and a business, then there's really no point in doing it.

Kim has no interest in stopping to smell the roses. Before a rose even finishes blooming, she is sniffing around for a new scent. I'm pretty sure that's how most billionaires approach life, so I'm not totally knocking it, but I would love it if Kim would enjoy what we have for a second.

Have you seen *National Lampoon's Vacation*? (If not, you should queue it up immediately after you've read this book.) There's a scene in which Chevy Chase as Clark Griswold starts to hurry his family away from where they are looking out at the majesty of the Grand Canyon because he just realized that he's accidentally stolen something, or his grandmother is dead. (I can't remember what it is—it's been, like, twenty years since I've seen it.) At any rate, he needs to get a move on. His wife, played by Beverly D'Angelo, asks, "Don't you want to look at the Grand Canyon?" So he slips his arm around her and looks out at one of the world's most spectacular views for a moment, taking it in, and then literally one second later, he nods his head twice, like, "Yup, got it," and immediately spins back around to go back to the car.

In our relationship, I'm Beverly D'Angelo and Kim is Chevy Chase.

I feel very fortunate to have the relationship and the family I have. While I come across as supremely confident on the surface, there are parts of me, and probably of every man, that say, "I don't know if I'm good enough for this situation that I have been given." When Kim races ahead of our life like that, it's like she's disappearing from this moment, this life we've built, and looking for something better, which leaves me feeling . . . alone.

So when she asked about writing a musical on top of everything we already have in the hopper, I wanted to know, *Why isn't what we have now good enough? Are you going to leave me behind for something that is?* In response, my protest behavior was to shut down her dream with my dismissive comment.

KIM

To me, the crazy thing is, in my mind, I was doing anything but leaving Penn behind. I wanted him to come *with* me on this journey. And if he wouldn't do that, I wanted him to support me as I reached the summit on my own. In attachment terms, I wanted him to be accessible to me.

When I reached out to him and said, "I have this precious, precious baby dream, and I'm going to share it with you right now. Please don't drop it," I wish he had at least said, "Oh my gosh, that's amazing. What an interesting baby! I can't wait to see how it grows. We should totally do that. Together. It will be hard. We'll have to invest a lot of time, but it will be me and you against the world, babe." Even when I'm just holding his hand crossing the street, that's the feeling I want—that the two of us are in it together. Instead, it felt like I reached out my hand and he just swatted it away, like, "You're on your own, kid, and good luck with *that* crappy idea."

To me, Penn asking if that was the best use of time sounded like, "You are a woman with a small brain, and, as a result, I will discount and ignore every single one of your ideas."

This is an example our most common fight. I have an idea, Penn shoots it down, and then I shut down. It's so common that I do this pantomime of clay pigeon–shooting every time it happens. I say my idea, Penn nixes it, I yell "Pull!" and then I act like I'm taking aim and exploding my idea. *Chck chck pooooh!*

When I brought up the idea of producing a musical, I knew the rest of the world would question my experience—I didn't need my husband to join in. I was also hurt that he didn't even understand why I was upset.

Intellectually, I know I can't expect my husband to jump off a cliff with me on every single adventure that pops into my brain, but deep down in my gut I would love if he got behind some of these ideas. Entrepreneurship and running a business are very lonely. You're out there in the wilderness, man, looking for someone to trust.

I can almost feel the protective shell that folds around my heart when it comes to trusting people. It's a physical response. My chest gets tight, my body shuts down, and I'm not capable of productive conversation. The moment I feel like we're in conflict, I want to armor up and walk out. I've heard this physical response is called an *intrinsic memory*; it's a kind of memory we store in the body, and I think I have a sense of where this one comes from.

My most memorable moment of putting on my armor was after my parents divorced. My mother and father were loving parents who tried their very, very best for twenty-seven years to stay married. But when I was in college, they decided: after five marriage counselors and several separations, they were finally calling it quits. I knew this was the best thing for them (for the record, I was right—they are both remarried and much, much happier), but man, it was hard. As they went about divvying up their possessions, they decided Dad would keep the house.

I went home for Christmas that first year after their split. My mom had always been the one who spent weeks decorating for the holidays; it was like her hobby was Christmas. Every year, every family member would get a new ornament, and anytime she went on a trip or to a special event, my mom would shop for an ornament to mark the occasion. There was a tiny ballerina from the year I started dance, a small manger scene (complete with miniature Jesus) from the year I played Mary in the Christmas pageant, a Miss Piggy from the year I was obsessed with the Muppets. Our tree was like a 3D, pine-scented scrapbook. My mom didn't stop at the tree. Garlands hung over doorways; tabletops were filled with pieces from her wooden Santa Claus collection. It was a freaking winter wonderland. Somehow it never seemed overwhelming. It just seemed like home.

When I walked into what was now my dad's house, it felt like I was walking into a stranger's home. My dad had tried his best to decorate a tree with the red and green balls he bought from the drugstore the day before, but to me, the tree looked naked. The tabletops were bare.

I tried my best to keep a smile on my face because I knew my dad was trying his hardest to make it special, but after an hour or so, I excused myself and curled up in a ball in the tiny closet of my former room. After muffling some sobs into a pillow, I wiped away the mascara stains and went back down to drink some eggnog. Home was gone. I was on my own.

You know when you take that big steep dive on a roller coaster? That's how it felt, as if I were floating, falling, and unsure of where I would land. Everything that had been home for me just *wasn't* anymore. It sucked. Since then, I've worked hard to bury any pain that came from my parents' divorce, and I wasn't going to let anyone put me in a situation where I would be sitting on the floor of a closet crying ever again. It became part of my pattern. When I was faced with fight, flight, or freeze, I chose flight. For years, I did what Penn calls "pulling the rip cord." My way out of an argument was to just inflate a parachute and jump out of harm's way. That was my protest behavior—when that lonely feeling would start to cast its shadow over me, I'd split.

In the car that day, I felt so shoved aside and diminished and alone that I couldn't actually form words. I knew any sounds that came out of me would be crying sounds. So I dealt with it the most effective way I knew how—I bounced, and then I refused to talk to Penn.

BEING PASSIVE-AGGRESSIVE IS REALLY AGGRESSIVE

Christopher told us that anytime you're passive-aggressive with somebody, it erects a wall between you and that person. On top of that wall is a ginormous sign flashing "I am not available to you right now." When you deflect and move on with your life—you pick the kids up, you make dinner, you watch TV—while giving your partner the cold shoulder, each of those actions signals, "You are not on my radar. You're on your own." Guess if that builds a feeling of secure attachment. (It does not.)

PENN

When Kim pulled the rip cord that day, she *literally* left me alone. She knows I don't do well with the silent treatment, and I suspect she knows she can get what she wants by doing it. When she shuts me out, nothing gets done. There's no singing, no writing, no joy. I can pretend like I'm having fun with the kids, but they can always tell I'm bummed out. God forbid I have to be on camera, which I am every day. I basically cease to function. I am not good at feeling alone. Never have been.

My brother Dail is eighteen months older than I am. He has always been a big music and movie fan, and even when we were kids, he was quieter than I was. (I mean, everyone was quieter than I was, especially back then.) You know how on TV older brothers are always giving their younger brothers wedgies and making fun of their zits? Not Dail. While we were growing up, he was the opposite of every older brother stereotype I've ever encountered.

When we were kids, school came easier to me than to Dail,

and so did sports and talking to people. This part is really hard to write because I feel like a real d-bag about it, but I took all those advantages and threw them right in his face. I corrected him when he was working on math at home. When he brought friends over, I hung out with them to try to show how fun I was. I beat him at basketball every chance I had. I needed to feel superior, and that's how I did it.

At the end of eighth grade, he decided to go to a boarding school in Virginia. Our whole family drove to Virginia to drop him off. We played twenty questions all the way there. I looooooove twenty questions, and I rarely lost, especially with Dail, because I knew him so well. A couple times I guessed the answer on, like, the third guess. Conversely, I always made mine completely impossible so he could never guess it. Being right made me feel pretty good about myself, so I tried to keep up the game for the whole trip. Dail never said anything like "This is stupid" or "You're making yours too hard." He just played with me.

I don't remember our goodbye; I'm sure it was something like "Later, dude." Dail waved goodbye one last time and walked into his residence hall, and at first, I was quietly excited. After all, I was going to get all of the attention from Mom and Dad from now on. I couldn't wait. As soon as we got back in the car, I asked Dad to play twenty questions, and he just said, "No, thank you." The four-hour drive home with that empty seat next to me felt like ten hours.

I thought I was going to rejoice being the only child and getting more attention. But I realized that when I told a stupid joke, my parents didn't always laugh at it, though Dail always had. When I got in trouble for making a mess or dragging in mud, there was no one to share the blame, just me. I missed my brother. I felt terribly, terribly alone, and slightly panicked. What was I supposed to do all by myself?

That's the same feeling I got when I looked over at the empty seat belt flopping next to me when Kim bailed. I was overcome with a sense of panic. I had to fix it right quick. As I saw it, the only way to fix the situation was to apologize, which is my go-to move even when I don't think I've done anything wrong, just to get the fight over with.

So, yes, I apologized. And apologized again. And again. And again.

WHY "I'M SORRY" SUCKS

We've been trained to think of "I'm sorry" as a magic wand for fixing whatever is going wrong, but sometimes we use "I'm sorry" more like a weapon than a magic wand. We wave it around trying to hack away at the armor our partners have put on or the wall they have built around themselves. Many times "I'm sorry" doesn't address the problem at all. In fact, it can actually make it worse, particularly when your attachment feels threatened. How many times have you heard your partner say "I'm sorry" and known that what they were really saying was "Please don't be mad at me?" It's clear they aren't trying to alleviate your pain; they are trying to alleviate their own pain. That kind of apology doesn't bring you closer together. It just puts more distance between you, and your attachment feels less secure.

When Penn came at Kim with "I'm sorry, I'm sorry, I'm sorry, I'm sorry, I'm sorry," it was clear he didn't even grasp why his comment was so hurtful, and that only made her angrier. The wall "I'm sorry" builds can be every bit as hard to scale as the one silence creates. But—good news, friends—there are magic words you can utter to knock that sucker down.

THE SIMPLE SWITCH

As adults in romantic relationships, our needs are a little more complex than a baby's. It would be amazing if you could just scoop your partner up and give her a cuddle or make sure she's dry and she's had enough to eat (and those things are important, too, as anyone who has seen Kim hangry well knows). In a good relationship, loving partners do a thousand things a day to make their partner feel attached. The most effective, love-building actions, however, are the ones that let your partner know they are not alone. The best way we've found to show your partner you are there for them in a difficult moment is by deploying what Christopher calls the *Simple Switch.*

Remember in *Christmas Vacation* when Clark Griswold was in the front yard punting the reindeer and punching Santa because his ten thousand lights wouldn't turn on, and then Ellen went into the garage and flipped a switch that solved everything? (Wait. You *have* seen *Christmas Vacation*, right? Seriously, Chevy Chase movies are American treasures.) The Simple Switch is the relationship equivalent of fixing that overtaxed power strip. You flip it and your crisis immediately de-escalates.

It is as close to a magic bullet as anything we've encountered. The incredible thing is how, well, *simple* it is. Are you ready for those three little words? The Simple Switch is the statement "Tell me more."

When you ask your partner to tell you more, what they hear is "I'm here." That panicky feeling that results in protest behaviors dissolves. The Simple Switch is the antidote to the feeling of aloneness. It has the exact opposite effect of every protest behavior—it draws your partner closer to you, showing that you want to understand more about what they are going through instead of pushing them away to go it alone. You are saying, "I am with you, I am available, I am paying attention."

The Simple Switch is authentic. It's exploratory, it's curious, and it's comforting.

Your partner calls to say he is going to miss dinner because he has to work late for the third night in a row? Instead of spitting out "Fine!" before you hang up, start with "Tell me more."

Your partner hints that she might like another baby? Instead of, "What are you thinking? We are already stretched to the limit," say, "Tell me more."

Your partner makes you feel like she's always looking for something better? Instead of dismissing her, say, "Tell me more."

Your partner jumps out of the car and starts giving you the silent treatment? Instead of rapid-fire apologies, say instead, "Tell me more."

There are hundreds of ways to ask for more information. It isn't limited to "Tell me more." The important thing is that you are showing your partner that you are there with them and that you are paying attention. Here are other great magic words to draw your partner closer:

- Why is this important to you?
- You have mentioned this before; how did you get here?
- Can you explain to me why this matters to you so much right now?
- How long have you been thinking about this?
- Can you give me a specific example?
- What would that look like?
- Help me understand where you're coming from.
- I'm not sure what you're asking me. Can you ask it again in a different way?

If you don't want conversations to become fights, keep asking follow-up questions. The safest response, always, is to ask clarifying questions. Don't make assumptions; ask for more information. This is your person. This is your wife, your husband, your life partner, your bed partner, your parenting partner, your partner in heart and soul and spirit. Take the time to keep pressing those healthy buttons. Every time you ask for more, it builds trust. Just like every time a mother comes back into the room with a bottle when her baby is crying teaches the baby that she is a reliable caretaker, your interest in knowing more, in being accessible, nearby, and attentive to your partner's needs teaches them to trust you will be there for them in the future.

The Simple Switch Question Checklist

There's an art to asking for more information. Not every follow-up question applies. Before shooting off a question, ask yourself if your question is

- clarifying
- compassionate
- neutral or affirming
- curious
- sincere

FLIPPING THE SIMPLE SWITCH

KIM

After we described our Broadway blowup to him, Christopher helped us talk through what Penn could have said instead that would have kept me in the car. He suggested:

"I heard you say you want to write a musical. I've never heard you say that before. Can you tell me why this is so important to you?"

Or, "A musical? Tell me more. What would it be about? Have you talked to anyone about this?"

That would have changed the entire tenor of the conversation. I would have felt connected to Penn instead of waved aside. Note that Christopher did not suggest Penn say he thought writing a musical was a good idea—because Penn didn't; message received loud and clear—but at least these versions acknowledge the idea was important to me.

Since we learned about the Simple Switch, we've been putting it to use, and it is definitely working. It helps when Penn can sit patiently and ask productive questions without judgment. He can be supportive without being phony. Penn uses language that's inclusive and encouraging, and I think he's realized that just because he asks me to tell him more about an idea doesn't mean I'm going to drop everything and chase it down.

For my part, I have learned to pump the brakes a little and know that not every idea I have needs to be acted on right away.

PENN

I've been trying! I'll give you an example: this hamper that we're making.

One of Kim's (many) dreams is to make a travel hamper you can pack your dirty laundry in when you're on vacation. I love the idea of this hamper; I would run out to buy one if they were on the shelves today. But Kim's gone through three manufacturers, and none of them have been any good. We have a batch of prototypes in our garage where our car should go that are so flimsy they couldn't hold a piece of paper.

Between me and you, we could probably have bought a pair of midlevel Jet Skis for what we've sunk into this hamper. That's a very expensive hamper, and you can't even do wheelies—or whatever the water equivalent of a wheelie is—on it. (Hang on, I just looked it up, they're called . . . wheelies, even though there are no wheels! Life is fascinating. Okay, back to the hamper.) I can tell Kim's been feeling discouraged. She came up to me two weeks ago, holding another failed prototype with a hangdog look on her face. She sighed, "I'm not sure if this was the best idea."

She let her guard down, and she was really sad. I lit up. *Oh wow, I have a chance to comfort my wife and not say "I told you so."* Instead of rubbing her nose in it, I just said, "Tell me how you're feeling." She didn't pull the rip cord. In fact, she moved closer to me and let me hug her. Touch is not one of her love languages, so a long hug is a rarity. She stayed in my arms a nice long time. It was a very good moment of closeness, and it wouldn't have happened if I hadn't flipped Christopher's Simple Switch.

That is the evolved us. Next step, Jet Skis.

KIM

Evolved but not perfected. We want to be clear that this is very much daily work. Some fights we get through and we never have to really go down that way again because we've communicated well about it. But I am still the dreamer and Penn is still the rose sniffer, and the struggle is ongoing. However, we have found if we just reach out to hear a little more about the other person's thoughts, we don't feel so alone, and the protest behaviors can be kept to a minimum. My rip cord remains holstered—most of the time.

Map Your Fight

Try this the next time you have a fight with your partner. After you've cooled off from active to dormant volcano, write down as much as you can remember about what you said to each other. Then go back through and write what you were feeling underneath what you were saying. If you read music, the transcript is like the melody and the emotions are the chord progressions.

For example, our fight went like this:

Kim: What if we wrote a musical? (*hopeful*)
Penn: Do you really think that's the best use of your time? (*annoyed/anxious*)
Kim: leaves car (*dismissed*)
Penn: ?? (*abandoned*)

Look at the words you've recorded to describe your emotions. Do they describe a person who feels a secure connection to their partner in the moment? If not, rewrite your fight with a few Simple Switch questions inserted. Now do the exercise again. How did the tenor of the fight change?

Here's the beautiful part. Using the Simple Switch transforms conflict into something that helps you grow as a couple. By asking those follow-up questions, you're not just letting your partner know they aren't floating out there alone in the universe; you're starting to understand why they decided to become an astronaut in the first place.

PS: You may be wondering, *Are they writing a musical or not?* Now that we know how to talk about it, we talk openly about our hopes of creating a show for the stage. Stay tuned.

09

I CHEATED ON YOU . . . FINANCIALLY

THE FIGHT

PENN

Have you ever watched one of those Lifetime movies that opens with the husband coming home early to surprise his wife with flowers? You immediately sense that something is wrong when he goes to open the front door and it is unlocked. He shrugs, like, *Huh, that's weird*, and then he turns on the light and—*bum-bah!*—he spots a pair of men's shoes in the vestibule. He follows an increasingly intimate trail of clothing up to the bedroom, where he opens the door to find his wife in the altogether with another man. Flowers wilt.

As insecure as I can be on occasion, I have never once been afraid of that particular scenario. Not only do I know Kim loves me, but she would have to be an affair ninja to get away with it. There are only thirty-four minutes in any given day when we are apart, and during eighteen of those one of us is in the bathroom, so I have always thought I was in the clear. But then one day . . .

I came back to the house after school drop-off, and just after I hung up my coat, I heard a weird popping noise coming from upstairs, followed by one of those silences where you know whoever made the noise is frozen stone-still, trying to figure out if anyone heard it. *Wutza?* I made my way up the stairs and into our bedroom, where I found Kim kneeling on the floor surrounded by a mountain of open packages. She looked like Cookie Monster had had his way with a stash of Chips Ahoys, only instead of cookie crumbs, there were a million cardboard boxes scattered around her. My wife looked up from the pile of luxury goods she had just unboxed and grinned maniacally at me.

I had to hand it to her. She had nerve. We had *just* had a conversation where we agreed we should keep an eye on our budget and start putting some money away for the future. That budget did not include the fancy sweaters or cosmetics I saw before me.

She was busted. So busted. But that didn't stop her from trying out a few of our signature moves when we fight about money. In the span of five minutes, she deployed . . .

The Discount Gambit:

Penn: How much was that dress?

Kim: Well, normally it's a hundred bucks, but it was 50 percent off, so only fifty, but with fifty dollars of savings, mathematically it was essentially free!

The Redirect:

Penn: How much was that face cream?

Kim: It was 30 percent off, and it's super important to me. We are on-camera influencers now. My skin needs to look amazing if you want us to succeed in this business.

Penn: You still haven't told me how much it costs.

Kim: Hmmm?

The "Oh Yeah?":

Penn: *(picks up stray receipt)* You spent $20 on a pair of tights?

Kim: Oh yeah? Well you spent $100 on headphones!

Penn: Oh yeah? You spent $150 on a haircut!

Kim: Oh yeah? You spent $200 on sushi last month!

And so on. It was like the worst live auction ever.

I was ticked. More than that, I was hurt. It definitely bothered me that Kim had spent a bunch of money, but that wasn't what got to me. What got to me was that I'd been as blindsided and deceived as that cuckolded husband.

Man, I had no idea money could do that to you.

KIM

It looks bad for me, I know, but let me explain: I really, really wanted those sweaters.

My first job out of college I worked as a television news reporter. My starting salary was thirteen thousand dollars a year. After taxes, rent, and food, I was scrounging for quarters out of my couch to put gas in my car.

Slowly, very slowly, I started earning more money, but just when it seemed like I had a handle on my finances, I met Penn and we got married and moved to New York City. He was a correspondent for ABC Sports, and I was a reporter for *Inside Edition*. That sounds fancy, and the numbers looked great on paper, but dang, they want five dollars for a muffin in New York City. Our monthly rent was about a third of what I made in a year for my first job. It was not sustainable.

We decided to move to Raleigh, where everything, including muffins, was more affordable. We still weren't saving any money, but we were getting by. Then "Christmas Jammies" happened.

You may not believe this, but we had no idea you could make money off YouTube. We thought our holiday video card was a goofy jingle we'd send to our relatives, but to our surprise, it took off. After seventeen million views in December 2013, we got a ten-thousand-dollar deposit into our bank account. When I saw that number, I couldn't believe it was real. I thought we were going to get an email telling us that a Nigerian prince wired us that money. You guys, the girl who put tuna fish in ramen four nights a week in her twenties just made TEN. THOUSAND. DOLLARS.

To celebrate, Penn and I treated ourselves to a nice dinner, and we didn't even look at the prices when we ordered. If you've never lived near broke before, let me tell you something: this is a strange feeling. To order wine with a meal and not worry about the final tab? It was the first time in my life I had felt such freedom.

Not every one of our videos got seventeen million hits—not even close—but by a year or so later, we had hit our stride making people laugh online. I felt secure enough to buy a few new outfits for an upcoming trip. And I bought new skin cream—the stuff they sell at a department store, not the grocery store. Of course, I needed some new shoes to go with my new skin and my new outfits.

And while I was at it, I wanted some of those top-of-the-line work-out leggings, the kind that suck you in and shape your butt and cost more than our weekly grocery bill. Yeah, I wanted some of those. So I did it. I bought all the things.

I was still on a high from my online shopping spree when Penn approached me in the kitchen that night.

"Hey babe," he said. "I've been thinking—while things seem good now, we should probably start saving some money. Cool?"

Gulp.

"Of course," I told him. "Yes, you're so right, honey. Let's save the extra we have left at the end of the month for a rainy day. Great idea. Best idea ever."

Two days later, I was pacing near the front door trying to run interference on the UPS truck. I didn't want a stack of incriminating boxes on the front porch. Finally, the truck appeared with enough boxes addressed to our house that the driver had to make two trips to retrieve them all.

Now, a responsible wife would have done one of two things. She would have told her husband, "I just spent a crap-ton on things I don't really need. But I want them, so suck it." *Or* she would have returned the items and quietly moved the money into a savings account. I did neither of those things. I wanted my rear-shaping leggings, and I didn't want to explain them.

I don't have to tell you what happened next. I was caught red-handed. Penn turned on his heel and left me alone with my plunder—and my shame. I clawed my way out of the tissue paper and packing tape and walked downstairs. Penn was sitting on the couch looking straight ahead like he was in a daze.

In the saddest voice I have ever heard him use, he said, "Why didn't you tell me about the money you spent? Why did you lie?"

Oomph. Great question.

MONEY CHANGES EVERYTHING

The short answer is, talking about money is our kryptonite as a couple. A few years ago, at one of our earliest sessions with Christopher, he had us do a marriage inventory—a 150-question checkup to see how we were doing as a couple. Afterward, he gave us a readout of our results. We did pretty well on most sections, including intimacy, spirituality, and even communication. *High five us!* We were feeling good about ourselves, but then we got to our score in the section about money. We had flat-out flunked. Every other section had a reassuringly tall red bar, but you had to squint to see the sliver of red in the finances section.

Christopher tried to make us feel better by telling us it's extremely common to have a low score in the money section, but then Penn asked if any other couples had ever gotten a ten out of ten in finances, and Christopher admitted that, well, yes, many couples had. Just not us. Not by a long shot.

For years, we were terrible at talking about money. It was like we'd thrown all the tools we'd developed as a couple into a bathtub and electrocuted ourselves into silence anytime we had to talk about our finances.

We like to think we've come a long way since then. We've had plenty of bumps and brawls, but after a slog, we've reached a point where we are as comfortable talking about money as we are dancing in wigs.

In this chapter, we will

- help you understand why talking about money is so hard
- show you the connection between money and shame
- declare bankruptcy on perfection
- show you how to laugh your way to the bank (emotionally speaking)

But first, let's circle back to see how we got so turned around about money in the first place.

KIM

It can be tough to vanquish the ghosts of your financial past.

I didn't grow up with money. Before I go on, I want to qualify this by saying that comparatively my family was absurdly lucky. We didn't get everything we wanted but absolutely had everything we needed. There are millions of people who are far worse off, but in my household, things were definitely tight. My mom balanced the checkbook before going grocery shopping to see if we could get apples *and* oranges or just apples. My great-grandfather was a cattle farmer, so I knew times were tough if the weekly menu was hamburgers, Hamburger Helper, sloppy joes, meatballs, and then meatloaf—but we were never hungry.

My mother was a piano teacher before becoming a schoolteacher, but some of her piano students' families didn't pay on time, so one weekend each month we would drive around to collect. I would sit in the car, and my mom would have to walk up to the door and ask for the money that was owed to her. She had every right to do it, but woof, as a kid, it made me wish I could disappear into our car's upholstery.

One Christmas, I desperately wanted a Cabbage Patch doll, but they were expensive and in high demand. Moms and dads were standing in line overnight to buy them for their kids. My parents didn't have the kind of jobs where they could scoot out to the mall for an afternoon, and there wasn't a bunch of extra cash around. My family knew how much I wanted that toy, so my grandmother got a plastic doll head from the craft store and sewed it onto a body with dimensions identical to a Cabbage Patch doll's. If you squinted or if you were not an eight-year-old girl, it was a pretty good copy, but my discerning eye noticed immediately that the nose, instead of being round and bubbly, was pointy. It was obviously not a Cabbage Patch doll. When I play back the videotape of that Christmas morning in my head, I zoom in on the moment where I rolled my eyes at this disappointing gift just to torture myself. I think I knew it wasn't cool to care about the brand, but I did—and I kept caring.

Later on, in middle school, I was obsessed with getting a pair of Guess jeans with the famous triangle on the right back pocket. At the time, they cost more than fifty dollars, and there was a 0 percent chance my schoolteacher mother would hand over her hard-earned money for some denim with a logo. "I could make you a pair for one-tenth the cost!" was her famous retort, but I wasn't about to have a denim version of the Cabbage Patch doll, so I saved my allowance and purchased a knockoff pair of jeans. My jeans had the coveted triangle, but it was flipped upside down. When I noticed the difference, I was so embarrassed that I started hugging the wall with my backside when leaving class so no one could see my shameful rear end.

When I became an adult, I wanted to be able to go to a store and buy things without having to analyze a spreadsheet first to determine whether I could afford them. In the depth of my soul, I wanted to be the type of person who had money, the type of person who could buy face cream and sweaters and leggings. So when I finally had my chance, I took it. I pressed the "purchase" button again and again. When I opened the boxes, the clothes were so beautiful. They came wrapped in tissue paper fastened with embossed stickers. Having the freedom to buy what I wanted was glorious.

PENN

Did what Kim just said make sense to you? Me too!

I can relate hard to the Guess jeans thing. My version was the famous Michael Jackson jacket that had the ridiculous number of unnecessary zippers. It seemed like every kid in the neighborhood was sporting one the year "Thriller" came out, and all I wanted was to be able to join the army of little Michaels. That was not in the cards for our family. The clothing my brother and I wore was 90 percent hand-me-downs and 10 percent T-shirts from our sports teams. My most treasured possession was a Tony Dorsett NFL jersey my parents gave me for Christmas. It's what made me a Cowboys fan, and a lifelong football fan. I remembered it being shiny and beautiful and perfect, and I wore it everywhere. When I was about thirty, I found an old photo album and a picture of me sitting on the floor with my best friend watching a Cowboys game. I was stunned when I looked closer to see my treasured jersey was a plain blue T-shirt, about two sizes too large for me, with undersized, uneven, ironed-on white letters that said C-W-B-O-Y-S. (The "O" had fallen off.) I should have known my parents didn't have the money to blow fifty bucks (or whatever it cost back then) on an NFL jersey. When your dad is a preacher (and not the kind who drives to a megachurch in a Mercedes), you get by on the kindness of others a fair amount.

I didn't get that jacket the year everyone went as MJ for Halloween. Or the year he was doing Pepsi commercials. But sometime around his "Man in the Mirror" era my parents found a jacket in a bin on the side of the road and gave it to me. I'm sure I thanked them, but I looked around and no one else was wearing that jacket anymore, so I didn't want it.

Around that same time, I got obsessed with tennis. I don't know how we ended up with HBO—I am positive we didn't pay for it, so maybe it was a promotion?—but I had started watching Wimbledon, and I was hooked. I didn't even own a tennis racket, and I certainly hadn't taken a lesson, but I loved picturing myself owning the court like Agassi. We lived right by a fancy tennis club, not more than a hundred yards away. I could sit on the couch by the window and watch all my friends slinging their rackets over their shoulders as they headed to the club looking like the popular boys in John Hughes movies. I would have given my left arm to play a match on those pristine courts. I know what it's like to want what it seems like everyone else has.

That's why I couldn't understand why Kim couldn't come out and say to me what she just explained above. She knew I came from similar circumstances. Why did she feel the need to hide (poorly) the spoils of her shopping? By the way, if she had broken down those boxes and neatly stuffed them in the recycling, she probably would have gotten away with it. But unfortunately for her, Kim suffers from a serious case of TUB FIRE (Thinks Unbroken Boxes Fit Inside Recycling Easily) Syndrome. She *never* breaks down boxes after she opens them. TUB FIRE is real. I am doing a 5K to raise awareness.

Her deception really threw me for a loop. What did she think was going to happen? Was she afraid I was going to go into beast mode? That I would become a raging monster who punched walls and threw things? Or was she scared I would try to tear her down verbally and make her feel small? How had we reached a place in our marriage where she felt she had to lie to me?

SPEND YOUR VALUES

As we were working through our issues talking about money, Christopher shared this joke with us: A couple goes in to visit a priest for premarital counseling, and the priest sits down with them to tell them what they can expect during their time together. He explains, "You might find some of these sessions difficult. We're going to talk about the fact that you both come from dysfunctional childhoods." The couple moves closer together on the couch so they can hold hands. The priest goes on, "We're going to talk about your relationship to God." They nod as he continues, "We're going to talk about the value of a healthy sex life." They blush furiously, but smile and nod again. Finally, the priest says, "And we're going to talk about how you spend your money." As soon as they hear that, the couple jumps up to leave. When they reach the door, the wife-to-be says to the priest in a huff, "You didn't tell us this was going to get *personal*."

Talking about money does feel really personal. It's not just us. We have friends who will detail every moment of their very private medical procedure, and then suddenly get super interested in their phones when the conversation turns to salaries. But why? Christopher gave us a rather brilliant answer to that question. He told us that a budget is a moral document. He explained that how you spend your money is a direct reflection of your values. When you sock money away in a 401(k), you telegraph your need for security. When you say yes to every invitation to a big night out, you show that you value living in the moment. We signify what matters to us through the items and experiences we choose to buy. Private school, mason jars, carbon offsets, sensible shoes, dream vacations—they are all packed with meaning. How you spend your money might not be conspicuous consumption in the eighties sense of the word—where you deck yourself in diamonds to showcase your wealth—but it is a signifier to the world of who you are and what you value.

When you spend in a way that is out of whack with how you see yourself, it feels like wearing an ill-fitting costume—clumsy, uncomfortable, and hard to ignore. The flip side of the coin is that feelings about money are a lot less complicated when you spend it in a way that is in sync with how you see yourself.

Is That in Our Budget?

You've probably tried the exercise of making a monthly budget to decide exactly where every penny of your paycheck will go. Most people find this too restrictive and end up tossing that kind of budget aside in frustration. Try this instead. Write a values budget, a list of what is most important to you. You can either draw from the list below or come up with your own. This is as important and foundational as it sounds, so treat it accordingly. Go for a meandering walk or drive by yourself before coming together with your partner for a dedicated discussion. Then rank your most important values one to ten. These values should help you determine where you spend the majority of your money. For example, if health is one of your values, go ahead and sign up for the premier gym membership or buy the organic milk. But if your friendships are higher in your top ten, buying a plane ticket to go visit your college roommate might trump the gym membership. Keep this list somewhere easy to find so you can use it as a filter to decide what is worth spending on—and what is worth fighting about.

Stability
Future security
Sanctuary
Family
Friendship
Compassion
Human connection
Convenience
Health
Fitness
Justice
Fun
Discovery
Travel
Style
Personal growth
Environment
Spirituality
Solitude
Time
Arts
Beauty
Freedom

PENN

I'm not perfect when it comes to money. I have spent the equivalent of the GDP of a small island nation on replacing lost wedding rings (yep, you read that right), but I actually feel pretty good about the way I'm using my funds most of the time. As you know, I'm a *carpe diem* kind of guy. I don't have a lot of interest in owning possessions that are going to fill up my home. Kim is just going to yell at me to pick them up off the floor anyway. I don't splash out on fancy watches or suits—I'm not even sure where I would wear either of those these days unless it was as a prop for one of our videos. I don't accumulate stuff. I buy experiences.

My biggest indulgence is food and beverage. I will order the steak and a nice glass of wine when we go out. Once a week, I will go out for sushi by myself and not stop eating until I'm full—and I'm six and a half feet tall. I can eat *a lot* of sushi. But I savor every bite, and I do it noisily, moaning and exclaiming "Uh! That is *so good*." I am always surprised when none of the other customers makes the I'll-have-what-he's-having joke. There is nothing more ephemeral than the pleasure of eating something delicious. It goes into your body and then out your butt in a very short period of time, but sitting there eating it (not the second part) is a real stop-and-smell-the-roses moment for me.

Remember how I told you I used to press my nose up against our window as my friends went to the tennis club? Guess what? As you know from chapter 6, I recently took up tennis! I started playing in my forties, and I love it. I can finally do the thing I wanted so much as a kid, and I don't feel guilty about it because being healthy is important to me and so is having time to socialize with my friends. Tennis fits my values budget.

The other major thing I purchase is time. When you run a small business out of your house, you have to treat that house like an office. Things need to run efficiently, and you need to have at least a semblance of order or nothing gets done. We have an assistant named Desmond who comes twice a week and helps us set up shoots, does laundry, and makes sure that we are not living in squalor. You know how they have sister wives in *Big Love*? Desmond is my brother husband. He is worth every penny.

Christopher was right—spending my values feels good.

SHAME ON YOU

Somehow, no matter how much money you have, it never feels like enough. Christopher told us when he asks couples what their top concerns are during premarital counseling, 90 percent of the men respond that they fear not being able to provide for their families. If they are not providing, then what, they wonder, do they have to offer? When there is not enough money to go around, they feel shame.

Brené Brown—or Saint Brené, as we refer to her in our household—is a genius on the topic of shame. One of the most useful things she says about shame is that it is distinct from guilt. According to Saint Brené, guilt is when you feel bad about doing something that is out of character, like when a punctual person runs late to meet a friend and then feels guilty for making them wait. Shame is when you feel bad about something because you think it *is* your character, like when you forget a friend's birthday and berate yourself for being a thoughtless person. It is so common for us to amplify a single note of negativity in the echo chamber of our souls until it drowns out everything else we know about ourselves. For example, on the same day we got the offer to write this book, someone wrote in our podcast comments section, "I would love to hear Penn take the lead more," and "Kim, you say 'um' and 'ah' and 'whatever' a lot, and it's really driving me crazy." Guess which thing Kim incorporated into her self-talk—becoming an author or getting dinged for talking the way everyone else on the planet talks? Um. Ah. Whatever. Despite having just been offered the chance to *write a book*, she felt like a terrible communicator with nothing to offer.

Shame is the fun-house mirror that warps our thinking. Money leads to a lot of shame because of the connection between money and our values. If what we spend says a lot about who we are, spending that contradicts our core values can be painful. "I probably shouldn't have done that" can quickly morph into "I am weak."

As Saint Brené wrote:

> I define shame as the intensely painful feeling or experience of believing that we are flawed and therefore unworthy of love and belonging—something we've experienced, done, or failed to do makes us unworthy of connection.

Holy cannoli. Unworthy of love? Unworthy of connection? No wonder we go to such great pains to hide when we feel ashamed of something we've done—like spending money in a way that doesn't fit with what we claim are our values.

KIM

"Unworthy of love" sounds about right to me.

Sitting on that closet floor, I burned with the shame of wanting to be the person who bought the fancy, brand-name thing. I wasn't twelve years old anymore. I didn't own a lot of name brands. Most of my clothes came from Target. (No shade on Target—I have spent so much of my life there I can literally shop the store blindfolded. Google "Kim Target blindfold." You're welcome.)

I had always resented people who seemed to get things through no effort at all, through luck. Growing up, my parents had worked so hard for what we had, and I have always prided myself on my strong work ethic. So when we got that "Christmas Jammies" money, in the blink of an eye Penn and I had a fat bank account. I couldn't get it through my head that we *had* worked hard for that ten thousand dollars. While "Christmas Jammies" might have seemed like an overnight hit, we had absolutely put in our sweat equity learning how to do video production and being on camera and corny dancing before it got a single view.

But even if I *had* accepted that we had earned that money, I couldn't believe, when I had options for what to do with it, I didn't spend it on groceries or opening a school in Haiti or even saving it for the future; I spent it on a very cute sweater (or three—okay, fine, six). For *moi*.

When Penn busted me I was ashamed that I was acting like that person I'd been jealous of in the seventh grade. I was also embarrassed that I just didn't have the wisdom or ability to save money. Let's be clear: no one was making me feel bad about wanting to own something nice. Even when I was younger, no one had ever said boo to me about my non–Cabbage Patch doll or my mom asking for money from her students or my wannabe jeans. The shame was all completely in my head. The person judging me was *me*. The call was coming from inside the house, which made it all the more horrifying.

When I am honest with myself, though, my worst feelings that day came from lying to Penn about it. Why did I feel the need to paper over my mistake?

DECLARE PERFECTION BANKRUPTCY

Who hasn't tried to pull the wool over their partner's eyes on occasion? It is natural to try to make yourself look good in front of the person you love. Maybe you suck in your gut or spend hours on your makeup routine or tweak the script a little when telling a story to make yourself seem wittier or more virtuous than you had been in the moment. Totally normal. And yet acting like you *never* screw up is insulting to your partner. First of all, ain't nobody perfect. Your partner already knows that. When you front like you are and make them pretend to believe it, you are asking them to be complicit in your phony-baloney act, which, when you think about it, is a rotten thing to do. On top of that, walking on eggshells around your partner implies that you think your relationship is too fragile to carry the weight of a little imperfection.

Sometimes people refer to the "curse of low expectations," but when it comes to relationship perfectionism, low expectations can be a blessing. One of the things we wish we had written into our wedding vows was a promise to cut each other some slack, to acknowledge that the other person is a flawed, bumbling creature just trying their best to get it right every single day.

It's time to declare perfection bankruptcy. It might sound silly, but just acknowledging the tiny mistakes you make daily can be great practice for copping to a more significant fail. Every time you fail, whether it's using salt instead of sugar in your coffee or forgetting someone's name, make a practice of telling your partner about it. When they don't head for the hills—and they won't—it sends a signal to your subconscious, *Oh, look, this one loves me even though I am not perfect.*

We've found that the key to preventing a goof-up from becoming a shame bomb is to remind ourselves that no single action defines us. Practice saying, "I blew it" or "I screwed up" or "I failed" instead of "I can't do anything right" or "I suck" or "I'm an idiot." As a partner, it's totally okay to acknowledge the mistake—"Whew, yeah, you did"—as long as you focus on the blooper, not the bloopee.

Become an Investigative Reporter

Next time you find yourself feeling so bad about something you did that you want to hide it from your partner, try this. Report what happened in the most dispassionate way possible, the way a journalist would. Any word that includes a value judgment—*stupid, foolishly, numbskull, a-hole*—gets the editor's red pen, as does catastrophic thinking. Instead of writing a scorching hot take on yourself—"I am such an idiot. How did I not see that Subaru in the parking lot? Am I blind? Now I've ruined the car, and we'll never be able to afford a new refrigerator!"—simply state the facts and do it in the third person: "A thirty-four-year-old woman pulled out of the Whole Foods parking lot and didn't see the Subaru waiting for her spot. She dented her fender, and it will cost five hundred dollars to fix it." Imagine reading the facts-only version. What would you have thought if you had come across that story in a newspaper (besides *Must be a slow news day*)? Maybe *That was careless*. Or *Ouch, that's an expensive hit*. Probably not *That woman is worthless*. If you can withhold judgment about a nameless stranger, don't you think you owe it to yourself to do the same when you make a mistake?

KIM

Lucky for me, I have had plenty of chances to admit I screwed up.

Last summer, it happened again. I impulsively blew the bank on something indulgent. When we were on a trip to California, we stumbled upon a pop-up store in the mall selling fancy face cream. The briefest of micropauses as we were walking by was all it took. The salesman had cast his spell on me. Before we knew what was happening, he dabbed some lotion on each of us.

Penn was having none of it. He looked at me and said, "I'm out. I'll be over there at that sports bar watching golf."

I could have gone with him. I *should* have gone with him. But this cream. . . . It was probably made by milking tears from baby dolphins, and it probably caused cancer, but I did not care. The wrinkles under my eyes smoothed out like someone had blown up a balloon under them. I had no more under-eye circles, just the gorgeous, well-rested skin of a funemployed twentysomething. It was magic in a tub. It was also insanely, insanely expensive, but I decided on the spot that it wasn't that important that my kids go to college. Reader, I bought it.

It was $750, and I bought it.

When I tucked the receipt in the bag, my whole body was trembling. That little tiny bag held a product that cost more than I made in three weeks at my first job. We have had cars that had a trade-in value of less than $750. *OMG, OMG, OMG.*

I could feel myself teetering on the edge of a vortex of shame, so for a good sixty seconds, I repeated in my head, *This decision does not define me.* I marched myself next door and strode right up to Penn and did that thing where you are half-talking, half-laughing and said, "Penn, I just spent $750 on face cream." He looked at me and said, "I'm sorry, what?" He took some deep breaths. But before long, he was laughing too. That was it. No blowup. No screaming. No shame.

It was like night and day from what had happened in the closet. I felt foolish, but not like I had moral leprosy. (I should tell you that I returned the lotion, so when you see that I still have deep under-eye wrinkles, you'll know why.)

PENN

I could tell how bad Kim felt. The whole thing was so ridiculous. The store was such a fly-by-night operation. It still read "Mandy's Ice Cream" over the entrance. I swear the impossibly gorgeous man who put the cream on our faces had eyelids that blinked the wrong way, like a reptile. When Kim walked into that sports bar all giddy and sheepish, it was clear she already knew buying the lotion had not been a good decision. More importantly, she trusted me—and our relationship—enough to come clean. The only option I had was to laugh at the situation.

THE BEST MEDICINE

Christopher will tell you that laughter is a sure sign of a healthy marriage.

Humor is our *lingua franca*. Laughter is at the heart of our business; it is also at the heart of our family. If we had to make a bumper sticker embodying our philosophy of life, it would say "Ha!" Laughing at life's absurdities is the way we bond. As we were putting together this chapter, we did some thinking about why that is, and Penn hit on something that felt true. He pointed out that when you are laughing together, you're pointed in the same direction, understanding things in the same way. Laughing at a situation draws you closer to each other.

The best humor gets at a profound truth—the frailty of the human condition. In everything from slapstick—we fall down sometimes!—to sophisticated, layered jokes about our insecurities, what makes us laugh deepest and hardest is the gap between what we want to be and who we are. We're all just puppies trying to crawl our way up onto a too-high couch—scrambling, occasionally triumphant, but frequently thwarted. When you can see your partner with compassion for the effort they are expending to do their best, it is harder to be a jerk. Laughing together, especially in times of stress, says to your partner that you're right there next to them trying to scramble up onto the sofa. And hey, maybe if you work together you stand a better chance of succeeding.

We encourage you to laugh more at life and to do it with your partner. While it may not always be easy in a tense moment to remember life's absurdities, we've found that some gentle barbs about past failures can prime the pump. Laughing at past mistakes has a way of diminishing their power, like when a kid laughs at a bully instead of getting defensive. Even the sharpest insult goes dull in the face of laughter. In our lives, we've done that with Kim's shopping spree. We refer to it as Boxageddon. We'll make a joke that she would have gotten away with it if it weren't for those meddling boxes, and we make cracks about TUB FIRE. Each joke shaves away a little more of the shame.

KIM

Before Penn, I would definitely spiral when I felt I wasn't living up to my—or someone else's—idea of who I should be. But this guy I married, when I am a stress case, will crack a joke and it's like someone hits a release valve on whatever pressure I'm feeling to live up to an impossible standard.

Like last spring, when we were preparing for a big trip and we were on each other's last nerves. We were going away without the kids, and planning it was like preparing for a hurricane to hit. We had to put away meals, arrange alternate transportation, and make contingencies in case medical supplies ran short. At the same time, we were in the midst of hiring a new employee, so a strong current of tension about money was running through the house as well. In a fit of ambition, we had also scheduled a photographer to come that same week to take some pictures for our social media accounts and our website. In my head, we would appear stunningly attractive and totally in love in these photos. You see where this is going, right?

During the shoot, we needed to look like we really liked each other, but we were *not* liking each other. Our whole deal is how we are a flawed but loving couple. We were nailing the flawed part. Loving? Not so much. I was giving myself face hemorrhoids because I was straining so hard to smile, but it was obvious to the photographer that he was going to have to step in. He asked, "Could you maybe sit a little closer together, maybe not on opposite ends of the couch? Could you maybe put your hand on his, just touch him in a way that doesn't look like you're afraid of catching something?" I moved exactly one inch closer to Penn. I swear it was all my body could handle at the moment. There was, like, a force field preventing me from touching my husband.

Penn could see I was struggling, so he looked at me and said in this smarmy voice, "Hey, girl. Later you want to go mash our private parts together?" I lost it. It was the way he said it out loud in front of a stranger. Every laugh that came out of my mouth helped me to relax. I loved that Penn had acknowledged that what we were hoping for and what we were getting were miles apart. Also, he said *private parts*. When you look at the photos, you can see the progression as we went from super tense, to about to pop, to an explosion of laughter, followed by love. We got some of my favorite shots of us as a couple that day.

10

WHY ARE YOU BEING SO SNIPPY?

THE FIGHT

KIM

Please don't judge us. Anyone who knows us can confirm that Penn and I are totally churchgoing, God-fearing people who love Jesus, but . . . we also love the explicit rap music from our youth. When we hear a song by A Tribe Called Quest or Missy Elliott or, best of all, Snoop Dogg, it sets something loose in us. And that is why, while most parents would be swaddling their little angels in blankets made of pure love after our church's Christmas pageant last year, we planned to rush out the back door of the church so I could change from my below-the-knee plaid dress into skinny jeans and a clinging-to-my-youth shirt before we headed to see the D-O-double-G in concert.

It was going to be a big night for us as a couple. Snoop was playing one of those intimate venues where there are no seats; you're just dancing and rapping along the whole time. I *love* going to that kind of show with Penn. We push up as close as we can to the stage and do that manic scream-singing thing at each other's faces, which is hard to do because we are smiling so wide. I was really, really looking forward to the show.

But first, we were going to enjoy a whole other kind of high at the Christmas pageant. The moments I sit with my butt in that pew, listening to those sweet, squeaky voices sing is the highlight of my year. We had just fought our way through the holiday season from hell, and I was ready to exhale and let myself be enveloped by peace and hope, and maybe a little incense. As we took our seats that evening, the organ was playing a quiet prelude and the candles glowed on the altar. *Ah,* I thought, *let the magic commence.* The program was about thirty seconds from starting when my husband leaned over and whispered to me, "You know, you've been really snippy lately."

Say what? Snippy? Me? The man was lucky we were in church.

In a low growl I snarled, "What. Are. You. Talking. About?"

He replied, "Well, you've seemed really mad at me all the time lately. It's like I can't do anything right anymore."

Smoke billowed out of my ears like I was an angry cartoon character.

"When? When have I seemed mad at you?" I demanded. I wanted facts and evidence.

But before Penn could respond, the opening notes of "Once in Royal David's City" pealed through the church. While I should have been blissed out, instead I was seething through the whole program.

I kept it together enough to take pictures after the performance and then somehow managed to get the kids home to pass them to the babysitter. I called a car to pick us up, fuming to myself the whole ride, *Snippy? Oh, you haven't seen anything yet, baby.*

About fourteen seconds after our Uber dropped us off in front of the concert venue, I turned to Penn and screamed (a real scream this time, none of this stifled we're-in-the-house-of-the-Lord stuff) "WHAT DO YOU MEAN, I'VE BEEN SNIPPY?"

I "apologized" if I wasn't meeting him at the front door like Donna Reed each night, but I listed five things that needed to be dealt with in our lives that were emergencies at that moment and told him, "These are the craps I have to give. I have this one, this one, this one, this one, and this one. I have zero craps left to give for you. Zero."

He looked like I'd slapped him, but he yelled back, "Okay, I get it. You don't care about me."

We could hear Snoop taking the stage inside, but by that time, I was crying and shaking with anger. As much as I'd been looking forward to that night, I realized I could not stand next to my husband for one more second pretending everything was fine. I called another Uber to come take me home. Alone.

PENN

One of the great things about this book is that you can see it from both perspectives. Isn't that amazing? Can you tell I am gritting my teeth and forcing a smile while I'm writing this?

Snoop Dogg is my favorite artist—maybe of all time. I got in on the ground floor with him when he was doing *The Chronic* with Dre. I love him. I had always wanted to see him live, and I wanted to do it with my wife losing her mind by my side.

Let's back up to the part of the night where Kim says that I leaned over to her and said, "You've been really snippy lately." Respectfully, I would like to add *lots* of extra context. We had been in productivity overdrive the whole month: running a business, raising children, fulfilling the typical holiday obligations, and, oh yeah, moving and selling everything my parents ever owned. And because we like to make things complicated, we thought it was a good time to add a puppy to the mix. We weren't getting consistent sleep, and I knew that earlier that day Kim had spent two hours cutting poop (the dog's) out of a shag rug. We were spent, and it was starting to show.

In the forty-eight hours leading into what should have been a peaceful moment inside the church, Kim had become increasingly irritable. She had snapped at me in the car when I was trying to help her with a moving issue, and she had accused me of not listening to her when I asked questions. At the same time, I couldn't help but notice that she continued to show incredible patience to everyone else—the kids, the people at the moving companies, the staff at my parents' nursing facility, the hundreds of strangers who were buying my dad's furniture to help pay for his healthcare costs—she was an absolute saint to everyone. Except me.

I leaned over and asked her if she was okay. Here I will cop to some subtext, specifically, *Why aren't you being nicer to me?* She made a bit of a face and said, "What do you mean? What makes you think I am not okay?" That was the moment when our night fell apart.

Intellectually, I knew Kim was exhausted, but in my heart, all I could feel was my wife treating me poorly. So, yes, I said, "You've been really irritable lately." She remembers "snippy"; I remember "irritable." (You say "potato"; I say "watch your step.") At any rate, everything changed. Her body language, her eyes, her voice, her everything. She was off to the races, whisper-shouting things like

"How dare you?" and "Oh, so you just expect me, after all that we are going through, to be super cheery and bring you a potpie and a martini every night?" (A potpie? We have literally never had a potpie at our dining room table, though it did sound delicious.)

Then she did that thing that I hate: she asked for specific examples. I am never ready for this. When I try to give her examples she often dismisses them, or says, "Okay, that's one. Is that all you've got?"

Before I even had a chance to come up with anything, the pageant started. It was beautiful. We held hands the entire time and smiled lovingly at each other as our youngest sang a spot-on solo verse of "Joseph Dearest." Surrounded by the love and optimism of beautiful nine-year-olds performing the Christmas story, our anger subsided.

Also, the earth is flat.

We did *try* to put it aside, because, I mean, Snoop Dogg! But then the blowup happened in the parking lot, and it was clear that I was not going to see the Doggfather any time soon.

The only intelligent thing I did all night was get in that Uber with Kim. She wanted to be as far away from me as possible, but this was getting serious. It was our biggest fight of the year, and I did not want her to pull the rip cord, so I got in behind her and we continued to fight like Doggs.

I don't want to go through that ever again. How do I never go through that again?

THANKS A LOT

When Christopher heard about this fight, he immediately came back with, "It is not possible to say thank you too often in a marriage." Come again now? Thank you? We were talking about "Silent

Night" and "Gin and Juice," not Secret Santa. We didn't know where Christopher was going, but to humor him we went with it and tried to think back to the last time one of us had shown the other a little appreciation.

Are there crickets in December? We are pretty sure we heard some. With every minute that passed, the silence became more incriminating. We dug deep. Kim was like, "Oh wait! I said thank you when you said bless you after I sneezed when we were digging the ornaments out of the attic. Remember?"

We started to pick up on where Christopher was headed. Our relationship was suffering from a serious gratitude deficit, and we were paying the price.

There have been dozens of studies and articles documenting the link between practicing gratitude and increasing personal happiness, and we—okay, Kim—read all of them. She has even been known to utter the phrase *attitude of gratitude*. We fully buy into the premise that cultivating gratitude increases your overall happiness, but most of what we've seen on the topic focuses on the interior experience of *feeling* gratitude. What we learned from Christopher is how important it is to turn that inside out and focus on *expressing* gratitude when you are part of a couple. *Thank you* is a magic word. (Or two magic words. Whatever. Just focus on the magic.)

It's a point of pride for both of us that we know what we've got in each other, and we are deeply grateful for our marriage, but we're finally figuring out that it isn't enough for us to just *feel* gratitude for each other; we have to demonstrate our gratitude in observable ways so the other person *knows* we feel grateful. If we have said it once, we've said it a million times: your partner is not a mind reader. If you want them to know something, you have to communicate it.

Most of the magic words we've shared with you in this book have the power to transform a conflict in the heat of the moment—to take the stress level down a few notches so you don't have a heart attack midfight. The suggestions we'll provide in this chapter are more like preventative medicine for overall relationship health. We're going to encourage you to get into the healthy habit of showing how much you appreciate your partner.

Before we go further, we want to warn you that you won't find any suggestions for increasing intimacy in this chapter. In fact, the word doesn't even appear. *Au contraire*, we're going to tell you to treat your partner like a stranger and swap out some of that cozy one-on-one time for more out-having-fun time.

A lack of appreciation for your partner is like mold. It creeps in silently, and once it's there, it is a bitch to remove. By the time you see it, you've already got lung disease. It is a contagion worth taking steps to prevent because, as Christopher told us, showing gratitude is one of the best ways to convey that you respect your partner.

KIM

For the most part, I know Penn respects and appreciates me, but when we first started working together full time, there were moments when I felt like Cinderella trying to please her wicked step-mother. No matter how hard I tried, I couldn't do anything right. (Erm, where have I heard that before?) On one of our first shoots as a new video production company, I attached the camera to the tripod incorrectly. It doesn't sound like a big deal, but I couldn't get the camera off the mount to make adjustments, and it sent me into panic mode. Penn came into the room, and, *in front of the client*, he yelled, "Did you actually think a tripod works like this?" He made grunting noises of someone who is so mad they can't make their face form words. I wanted to crawl into the nearest hole and live out my days beneath the crust of the earth. Forward my mail; I no longer wanted sunlight to hit my face. I tried to laugh it off and crack jokes for the sake of the client, but I was pissed and demoralized. A colleague on the set whispered to me, "I can't believe you let him talk to you like that." Neither could I.

The ride home that afternoon was tense. The agony and embarrassment of being berated in front of our clients was compounded because Penn was in flat-out denial, so I did a petty—but effective—thing. I recorded him during another meeting so he could hear for himself how he talked to me. It was eye-opening for him. He looked at me in shock after the video ended and said, "I'm so, so sorry." He had been completely blind to his own behavior and how crummy it was for me to be on the receiving end of it.

EMOTIONAL BLINDNESS

The truth is we humans miss a lot when it comes to how our behavior affects our partners' emotional states. Don't get us wrong: with our highly tuned sensory systems, humans are perception monsters, and we still kick robot heinie when it comes to synthesizing our perceptions and processing emotions. But there are limits to how much information we can take in, and those limits have consequences.

We assume that if you know who we are, you own a computer or a smartphone. Maybe you've used one of those machines to check out the video of the Monkey Business Illusion, popularized by Christopher Chabris and Daniel Simons in their book, *The Invisible Gorilla*. If not, the title is a pretty big spoiler, but in the video, two sets of women wearing either black or white shirts pass a basketball to one another as a voice-over instructs you to count the number of times the players wearing white shirts pass the ball. Just as you're getting the hang of it, a person dressed in a gorilla suit comes out and does some quality chest thumping before exiting stage left. But get this: of viewers who were not warned to look out for the gorilla, more than half of the people watching the video failed to notice it. A gorilla! Viewers were so highly attuned to the counting, they missed the gorilla. This perceptual selection is called *inattentional blindness* or the *spotlight effect*. The gorilla didn't register because it was outside the spotlight of the viewers' attention.

As a scientific term, inattentional blindness pertains to stuff that goes on in your visual field, but as a metaphor, it pertains to how you're screwing up your relationship. If there is a high level of sniping going on in your relationship, ask yourself if you might be suffering from a kind of emotional blindness. We can take in only a portion of the emotional landscape in a given situation—whether it's missing a critical eye roll in a meeting because you are hyperfocused on your presentation or failing to notice your partner struggling because there is so much other stuff going on in your life. One of the most glaring emotional blind spots in most marriages, Christopher pointed out, is a lack of appreciation. That was certainly the shape our gorilla had taken that holiday season.

KIM

Now it's *my* turn to add some extra context.

That night in church was going to be like crossing the finish line after an emotional marathon. I was ready to let my pulse settle from "just below cardiac incident" to "resting heart rate." It had been a hectic few months. Penn's dad's health had taken a nosedive. One month he was driving to the store on his own; the following he was too confused to find his way to the kitchen. As Penn mentioned, we moved him from a place where he'd been living fairly independently to the same skilled-care facility as his wife so they could be near each other.

We arranged for movers, sorted through furniture, and put everything in boxes, all while dealing with the usual Christmas madness and the extra madness that comes from having a business that is particularly busy during the holidays. On top of that, I was chair of a committee at the kids' school and the big event associated with it was in December. Plus, my mom was in town to see the Christmas pageant, so I was hosting too. I just wanted to get to the finish line.

I am no stranger to finish lines, emotional or otherwise. In fact, I love a good footrace. A few years ago, I ran a charity 5K in honor of my aunt who died of cancer. I was four months postpartum, and I was in no condition to be running. It was only five kilometers, but to my still-healing body it felt like an ultramarathon. I was on track for a personal record (my slowest time ever), and I finally got to the point where I could see the finish gate about two hundred yards away. I had just started my final push, wrecked abs be damned, when the course officials *picked up the finish line and started moving it.* Someone figured out that they had measured the distance incorrectly. I wanted to collapse on the pavement and sob. I'd been giving it my all, panting the whole way, and now there was more road ahead? I couldn't believe it.

That was what it felt like when Penn hit me with the "snippy" remark that night in church. It was like he'd moved the finish line on me, and he didn't appreciate how much effort it had taken for me to get as far as I had.

PENN

If you had asked me that December, "Is Kim doing a lot right now?" I would have said, "I guess so? Probably? Yes?" But Kim *always* does a lot. Being capable is kind of her thing, like mine is being the good-times guy. She is a master logistics juggler and schedule maintainer, and she gets stuff done. Maybe that's why I didn't notice that underneath her checklists, calendars, and call logs, she was sucking wind.

Talking through our blowup with Christopher was like watching that video Kim had made of me all over again. I could see how I had neglected to thank Kim for all the extra work she was taking on with panache on top of her general all-around awesomeness as a partner.

KIM

As tempting as it is to let Penn shoulder all the responsibility here, the truth is, I wasn't showing him a ton of appreciation either. In times of stress, I am absolutely guilty of putting on a smiling face for other people but letting that mask fall around Penn and showing him my true ugly feelings.

I should have been more tuned in. After all, everyone I ran into during the time when the crisis with Penn's parents was most acute asked me, "How is Penn holding up these days? Is he okay?" And I would just say, "Don't worry about him. Penn is a rock." As we've established, my husband doesn't get that emotionally charged up about anything, but I should know better. There is definitely a lot going on under the calm surface.

I was so busy that I simply had not noticed that Penn was drowning. I was giving so much to other people that when he walked into the room, I wasn't making eye contact like I normally do. Or laughing at his jokes. Or smacking him on the rear when he passed me in the kitchen. At night, we weren't even sitting on the couch together watching TV. It was a horrible time for him, and I just wasn't there.

The impact that this emotional starvation had had on him became super clear once we got back to our house after we'd called it on Snoop. We were both still pissed, and we circled each other cautiously.

Finally, Penn said, "Do you want to know how I feel?"

Still furious at him, I spat out, "Sure. Go ahead. Tell me how you feel."

He replied, "My mom can't say my name. My dad hates me for moving him to a home. I am losing my hair from the stress. My dog has a hooded vulva so I have to stay up till all hours of the night to wait until she pees. I am exhausted. My wife may love me, but it sure doesn't seem like she likes me." He paused for a beat and then said, "I feel lonely."

As soon as I heard him say that, suddenly, I got it. He was going through all this stuff, and his wife hadn't been paying attention. He needed me to treat him with the kind of grace and patience I was showing everyone else, instead of kicking him to the bottom of my to-do list. I had been treating strangers on the internet better than I had been treating the person I love most in the world.

LIKE A STRANGER TO ME

We know a couple who has been together for nearly twenty years, and they still seem to be as crazy about each other as the first day they met. At a rehearsal dinner one time, we overheard a newly engaged couple ask them what their secret was. What they said was really simple: they try to treat each other with the same respect they would show a stranger. At the time, we thought, *Eh, our secret is more like Dorothy on the streets and Blanche between the sheets.* But after our session with Christopher on this fight, that advice made so much sense to us.

Sometimes you only have so much to give, and chances are, you give it to a stranger, not your partner. We let ourselves cut courtesy corners with our partners. How many times have you answered your partner's "How was your day?" with a quick "Fine," and then unspooled a list of chores that needed to get done? Or criticized the kind of cereal they bought instead of thanking them for doing the grocery shopping? Experts say this is because we trust our partners to love us even through our worst behavior.

If you have kids, letting it all hang out like this might sound familiar. When we used to drop our daughter off for preschool, she'd be screaming and pitching a fit so big when she got out of the car that we were constantly worried someone was going to call Child Protective Services on us. One morning when her hysterics had reached Real Housewives level, we were super apologetic as we dropped her off with her teacher. We handed her over like we were passing along a grenade with the pin pulled. As we started to apologize yet again for her behavior, her teacher looked at us like we were the type of people who pull grenade pins and said, "You do know it's because she loves you so much that she's acting like this around you, right? Lola is an angel for us." Hearing him say that was oddly reassuring. She felt like she could freak out around us because she trusted that we would still be there for her when she calmed down.

We agree that it is tremendously comforting to know that you don't have to put on a happy face all the time for your partner, but just because you feel comfortable enough to show all your roughest edges doesn't mean that you should. The line between comfortable and rude is razor thin, folks, and if you're not careful, those rough edges leave a gash.

Look at the statements below. Be honest. Do they better describe how you behave with a waiter or with your spouse?

- I smiled when I greeted them.
- I said thank you when they brought a glass of water for me.
- I asked for their opinion.
- I asked, "How are you today?"
- I made eye contact and gave them my full attention when they spoke.
- If they made a mistake, I politely pointed it out and was gracious when they fixed it.

If you fall on the waiter side of the equation, perhaps it's time to start treating your partner more like a stranger.

THANKS AGAIN

So what does that entail? For starters, think back to the two things your parents insisted you say to be polite: *please* and *thank you*. Nothing against please, but for our money thank you is absolutely magic. Even when you are in a crappy mood, saying thank you is pretty darn easy.

The best thank-yous are prompt and specific. Say it now and you won't give resentment over a lack of appreciation a chance to fester. All you have to do is note your partner's thoughtfulness. When you catch your partner in the act of doing something lovely, just say "Thank you" in that moment. That's the sunlight that prevents the first spore of resentment from blooming into a stubborn, toxic mess. There's no need to write a sonnet about how your partner did the best trash taking out that has ever been trash taken, but you should be specific with your thank-you so that it sticks. It's like writing a thank-you note for a present. "Thanks for the gift" feels cursory, but "Thank you for the wind chimes; it's like Tinker Bell lives in our tree now. Each time I hear them ring, I think of you and smile" shows real appreciation.

Here are a few examples of how to take a slapdash thanks and turn it into a real show of gratitude.

Scenario: Your partner cooked dinner even though it was your turn, because you had to stay late to take a last-minute phone call at the office.

Good: "Thanks for cooking."

Magic words: "You made such a great meal! I felt like I was eating in a restaurant only better because we didn't have to leave the house, and I didn't have to worry about picking something up on the way home or rush off my phone call."

Scenario: Your partner did the lion's share of the driving on a long haul while you zoned out.

Good: "Thanks for driving."

Magic words: "You drove for so long! All I did was sit here and scroll through my phone, which I desperately needed, while you stared at the boring road for three hours. I feel so much more relaxed now."

Scenario: At a dinner party, the talk turned to politics . . . and then turned ugly with one guest really coming at you hard before your partner stepped in.

Good: "Thanks for being cool about that."

Magic words: "You really had my back in there when Barry was being aggressive. I know you don't love getting in the mix when there is conflict. That took courage. I love having you on my team."

You might notice that these thank-yous take a similar form. Not only are they specific, but they highlight the sacrifice the person made as well as the benefit to you. Acknowledging both really drives home the point: *I appreciated that. I appreciate* you.

Here's a little Mad Lib you can use next time you're giving thanks (try not to use the word *butt* as much as you did when you did Mad Libs as a kid):

> Hey, thanks for *(verb)*. That must have taken a lot of *(noun)*. You saved me from having to *(verb)*, and it made me feel *(adjective)*.

No one gets sick of hearing those magic words. We'd be shocked if your partner doesn't stand a little taller and grumble less about chorin' if they know it will be appreciated. Stockpile those thank-yous. That way, when your partner goes looking for facts and evidence that they are appreciated, they'll have ample data.

Look Out for Good Behavior

Set yourself a goal of spotting good behavior in your spouse. Each time you notice something thoughtful or kind, write it down. You don't need to do a whole song and dance about how amazing they are for doing it. So many things go unnoticed that just noticing is enough. Then read your note out loud to your partner before placing that little piece of paper in a jar. Our guess is that the first few might take a while to note, but once you are programmed to look for thank-you-worthy deeds, you'll have a full jar before your partner can say "snippy."

GO PUBLIC

As people who are rarely more than twenty feet apart from each other, we get that it is not always easy to see your partner in a generous light and act accordingly. If you are having trouble mustering up the ability to be courteous to—let alone appreciative of—your partner, if every single thing they're doing is driving you up a wall, here's an idea. Spend less time with them one-on-one. Get out of the house. Go be together in public. You are less likely to snap at your partner if you are around other people. There's a herd immunity of civilized behavior pressuring you to keep your voice low and your tone respectful. There are norms that keep our anger, our anxieties, and our frustrations in check. Christopher guessed correctly that this is one of the reasons we love doing the podcast. It is a time where we are focused on each other, but because we are aware that every word we say is going to be heard by thousands of people, we try to talk to each other with respect.

We often bring our best selves out in public, so exposing your relationship to some sunlight will help you to be respectful and will show your partner in a more flattering light. A virtuous circle of appreciation can get rolling when you do this.

One of Penn's favorite moments with Kim was when she insisted that someone else treat him with respect in public . . .

PENN

I am tall. Tall is great for basketball and changing lightbulbs and, apparently, running for president. Tall is bad for airplanes and rock concerts.

Everyone knows that the best place to stand at a concert is in that big pit right in front of the band where you can see the set list on the floor and watch the sweat spread across the drummer's chest. But every time I go to the front I can feel the white-hot hatred of the people behind me boring into the back of my head. Even if I earned that spot by getting to the venue hours early, a steady beam of contempt pierces my skull once the show starts. Now, if you have read this book carefully, you know that my least favorite thing is having people hate me, so when I go to a show by myself or with my (also tall) brother, we stand in the back to avoid the spite. But Kim loves going to the front, and she wants me with her, so most of the time I oblige, as I did when we went to see the Dan Band a couple years ago.

We were milling around, drinking beer as we waited for the Dan Band to appear after the opening act. Before the band got on stage, this woman behind me started griping, "Oh, great. I paid a hundred bucks for this ticket and this beanstalk is right in front of me." I turned around and said, "I'm really sorry, I know I'm tall. I could try and squat a little" (which I did). She responded, "Your being sorry doesn't make you any less tall." Burn.

The band came out, and Dan started to sing his first song, but all I could hear was, "Ugh, I can't see anything!" While everyone was dancing their faces off, I was trying to hold my awkward squat. I was bent over far enough that this lady's mouth was at ear level when she said, "Still pretty tall up there aren't you, asshole?"

I whipped around and said, "You know what? I'm gonna go in the back by the bar." I left Kim with her friend Anne and made my way to the back of the venue.

About ten minutes later, the same woman walked toward me with watery eyes. What was going on? Had she been crying? She grabbed my hand and tried to pull me back into the crowd. I asked what she was doing. No lie, she said, "I need to get you back to the front of the concert or your wife is going to kill me."

When I got to the front, Kim gave me a big smiling hug and said, "We missed you!" The crying woman disappeared, and I had an amazing time.

After the show, in the car, I asked what had happened.

Before Kim could say anything, Anne answered, "Your wife went *off*, Penn. She started screaming at that lady, 'You have been extremely rude to my husband. Yes, he is tall. But he has a right to be here just like you do. He was also here first. He tried to be nice to you and you were really disrespectful. He's too nice to tell you that you are ruining his night, but I am not.'" How cool is that?

I maybe should be a little embarrassed that my wife had to stick up for me, but mostly I just felt loved. Kim had my back. We spend plenty of time taking each other for granted since we live together and work together, so her sticking up for me in public was worth its weight in gold.

PDA (PUBLIC DISPLAYS OF APPRECIATION)

If you want to take your thank-you game to the next level, praise your partner in public for something they have done. We do this as a society in a million different ways. There are Teacher of the Year awards, buildings named after charitable donors, applause after a great presentation, cheers at a basketball game, but so few times in a relationship do we make public note of how much our partner is contributing. When you are tuned in to the nice things your partner does and you take the time to tell someone else about it, it amplifies the impact of your thanks.

Become Your Partner's Publicist

Think of it as your job to market your partner as Best Spouse Ever. Promote an image of him or her as someone who does great stuff all the time. Here are a few ideas for spreading the good word:

- During a dinner party, tell your friends how hard you laughed at a funny story your partner told you earlier that week.
- While you're visiting your parents, tell them about a time your spouse changed your kid's throw-up shirt during a car ride without a word of complaint.
- Tell your kids how their mom spent all day filling out forms so they could go to camp and still managed to smile at you at the end of the day.
- When your partner opens the door to a restaurant for you, say to people around you, "Isn't she the best?"
- Put a "spotted" post up on social media where you caught your partner doing housework—the polar opposite of the great toilet paper shaming.

This December, we learned how right Christopher was. You can never say thank you too much. So when your spouse needs that gratitude, drop it like it's hot.

ONE LAST THING

PENN

You made it to the end of the book! Special shout-out to any dudes who made it this far. I am aware that many of you were tempted to ditch this book to go back to bingeing *Better Call Saul.* (No judgment; Bob Odenkirk is amazing.) Thanks for sticking around. It's possible the fact that you made it to the end of the book might lead to some gratitude nooky—so you're welcome for that—but hopefully that's not why you finished. Hopefully you really want to get better at this whole marriaging thing, and wanting to get better is the first step to getting better.

It took us more than three years to research, write, and publish this book, but this is the one part of it that I wrote in early 2021. (BTW, holy crap! COVID is still bleeping here.) And I have good news to share: some of this stuff is starting to sink in. For example, I am using the magic words now without having to go back and look them up. I am taking a mental chill pill and cooling down before I speak during a fight. I am asking for what I want instead of hoping that she'll just figure it out. It's all starting to come more naturally to me.

Also, we have been "doing more laundry." (If you don't know what that means, you need to go back to chapter 5.) Guys, it's amazing how much more often you can do laundry when there isn't some type of resentment brewing beneath her seemingly placid exterior.

We aren't in a "fight-free" environment, nor will we ever be, but the fights are more constructive. Bottom line, our relationship is in a better place than it was, even since we finished writing this book six months ago.

KIM

That is what happened for us. Not only do we bring out the best in each other but we've learned to come to the conversation assuming the best. I know too many couples who feel personally attacked every time a partner is late or didn't remember to fill up the gas on the way home. But I know now that Penn isn't trying to avoid me when he wants to go hang out with friends; he is a massive extrovert who needs loads of social time. And he knows I need alone time on the couch with a good book and doesn't get offended when I claim that time. Our fights became infinitely more productive when we both came to the table knowing we were both doing our best. (Except for getting laundry into the hamper; Penn is most definitely *not* trying his best there.)

In a functional adult relationship, I believe you judge your partner not for their shortcomings but for who they are at their core and how they love you. I love Penn for his ability to make me smile, his basketball-sized heart, and his unrelenting good cheer. If he never wrote another clever lyric again, I would still be grateful for him every single day of my life. And deep down, I know he feels the same way about me.

FIGHTING IS A LOVE LANGUAGE

It's a tall order to expect to be constantly attracted to and in harmony with a creature as complex as another human. Add jobs, kids, and family to the mix, and any relationship can tilt scarily out of balance. So why do we do it? Why do we link ourselves to one person for life? At the risk of being corny (too late?), our feeling is that marriage is the best shot we've got at keeping ourselves from falling into the void of feeling alone, unseen, and like we don't belong. Until scientists get those brain–computer interface webs up and running, talking to each other is the only way across that void, so our goal in this book has been to show you how to build a reliable bridge to connect you securely to your partner.

Our marriage is a living, breathing, unfinished, imperfect, constantly changing part of our lives, and no matter how deeply and completely we love each other, fighting will always be part of it. With every argument, we learn a little bit more about each other. With every resolution we show a little more of ourselves. We hope you've found something useful in our fights and the ways we've learned to resolve them. When you fight the right way, you become a stronger couple.

We've been using these techniques for almost a decade now. While we still mess up every single day, knowing that we have the tools to clean up the mess has made us a lot steadier when we do get into it with each other. We say what we mean and trust the other person will love us anyway—and we think that's worth fighting for.

ACKNOWLEDGMENTS

PENN

I must start by thanking my parents. They are currently in a skilled nursing home battling dementia, but man, they are crazy about each other. He's eighty-one and she's seventy-six, and he still grabs her butt. Seriously, they can't keep their hands off each other. They were great role models for an imperfect but successful marriage. I don't think they'd be able to read and understand this book in their current state, but their fingerprints are all over who I am as a man, a father, and a husband.

Thanks to my brother, Dail, who taught me about patience and grace, two things you must have to write, and abide by, this book.

KIM

I owe oceans of gratitude to my parents. I learned so much about marriage from watching them navigate a divorce. My mother and father worked hard, really hard, to make their partnership work. I want to thank them both for showing me the work is important. They both have a happy ending after finding and remarrying partners who fit them perfectly. Thank you both for inspiring me to pick well. And thank you to my children, Lola and Penn Charles, who were patient and proud as we worked on this book.

PENN AND KIM

Thanks to our editor, Becky Cole. If you've never written a book, here's a little secret: every editor's name should be on the cover. She took our hot mess and made it into something that we are very proud of. She hates that last sentence because it ends with a preposition, but we are leaving it in. (Haha, that one too!) Also, since we wrote this during COVID-19, we have no idea how tall Becky is. We are guessing five-foot-six.

Thanks to Matt Baugher and the team at HarperCollins Christian Publishing. Matt is letting us air all our dirty laundry. He gave us the time, support, and encouragement to create this book, and for that we are eternally grateful.

We make silly videos, but there is a hardworking team behind us that makes all that we do possible. Thanks to our HFAM team members, Ann Marie Taepke and Sam Allen. We often get the question "How are you guys so prolific with your content?" The answer is: Ann Marie and Sam. And, of course, Desmond Wilson, who keeps us on track, and Max Trujillo, who produces our podcast. Thanks to our manager, Larry Shapiro, who our children legitimately think is their uncle, which should say all you need to know. Thanks to our agent and dear friend, Byrd Leavell, who is just trying to have an awesome time. His positivity, guidance, and encouragement got us from "Hey, you guys should write a book," to the thing you are currently holding. Also, for someone we've gone to a million bars with, it's been great to see how good he is at his job. And an überthanks to our counselor and dear friend, Dr. Christopher Edmonston. Our book is 300 percent better thanks to him, and so is our marriage. He should also be on the cover, and on the couch, with us.

NOTES

CHAPTER 1: THE BATTLE OF THE BRA

7 **psychiatrist Bessel van der Kolk explained** Bessel van der Kolk, "Bessel van der Kolk: How Trauma Lodges in the Body," July 11, 2013, in *On Being with Krista Tippett*, podcast, MP3 audio, https://onbeing.org/programs/bessel-van-der-kolk-how-trauma-lodges-in-the-body/.

CHAPTER 2: CAN'T YOU JUST BE HAPPY FOR A MINUTE?

25 **"an undifferentiated family ego mass"** Mark Stanton, Irene Goldenberg, and Herbert Goldenberg, *Family Therapy*, 9th ed. (Stamford: Cengage Learning, 2016), 196.

27 **Researchers analyzed depression screenings** Amanda MacMillan, "Want to Feel Happy? Hang Out with a Friend in a Good Mood," Health.com, September 21, 2017, www.health.com/condition/depression/moods-are-contagious.

27 **Another study found that simply observing someone** Veronika Engert et al., "Cortisol Increase in Empathic Stress Is Modulated by Emotional Closeness and Observation Modality,"

Psychoneuroendocrinology 45 (July 2014): https://doi.org/10.1016/j.psyneuen.2014.04.005.

CHAPTER 3: CAN YOU PLEASE JUST SAY SOMETHING? ANYTHING? ANYTHING AT ALL?

50 **John Gottman identified stonewalling** John Gottman and Nan Silver, *The Seven Principles for Making Marriage Work* (New York: Harmony Books, 2015), 38.

51 **Purdue University professor of psychology Kipling Williams** Amy Patterson Neubert, "Professor: Pain of Ostracism Can Be Deep, Long-Lasting," Purdue News Service, May 10, 2011, https://purdue.edu/newsroom/research/2011/110510WilliamsOstracism.html.

53 **Psychiatrist and proponent of mindfulness Dan Siegel** Dan Siegel, "Dan Siegel: Name It to Tame It," video shared by Dalai Lama Center for Peace and Education, December 8, 2014, on YouTube, https://www.youtube.com/watch?v=ZcDLzppD4Jc.

53 **Researchers at UCLA** Michael Miller, "'That Tarantula Is Terrifying!': The Power of Naming Emotions to Reduce Anxiety," Six Seconds, updated January 21, 2018, https://www.6seconds.org/2018/01/21/getting-unstuck-power-naming-emotions/.

54 **Another UCLA researcher** Stuart Wolpert, "Putting Feelings into Words Produces Therapeutic Effects in the Brain; UCLA Neuroimaging Study Supports Ancient Buddhist Teachings," UCLA Newsroom, June 21, 2007, newsroom.ucla.edu/releases/Putting-Feelings-Into-Words-Produces-8047.

59 **"never to empty the well of my writing"** Ernest Hemingway, *A Moveable Feast: The Restored Edition* (New York: Simon & Schuster, 2014), 58.

CHAPTER 5: I'M STRUGGLING WITH SNUGGLING

88 **In psychologist Albert Mehrabian's famous studies** Allan and Barbara Pease, "The Definitive Book of Body Language," *New York Times*, September 24, 2006, https://www.nytimes.com/2006/09/24/books/chapters/0924-1st-peas.html.

89 **If you are in a relationship** Cindy Eckert, "Let's Talk About

Se . . . I Mean, Ice Cream," October 29, 2019, in *The Holderness Family Podcast*, hosted by Kim and Penn Holderness, podcast, MP3 audio, 39:35, https://theholdernessfamily.com/lets-talk-about-sex/.

CHAPTER 6: I NEED TO SEE OTHER PEOPLE

112 **Harvard professor of psychology Ellen Langer** Susan Weinschenk, "The Power of the Word 'Because' to Get People to Do Stuff," *Psychology Today*, October 15, 2013, www.psychologytoday.com/us/blog/brain-wise/201310/the-power-the-word-because-get-people-do-stuff.

CHAPTER 7: ARE YOU EVEN LISTENING TO ME?

127 **One study from the University of Arizona** Julie Hyunh, "Study Finds No Difference in the Amount Men and Women Talk," University of Arizona Undergraduate Biology Research Program, June 19, 2014, ubrp.arizona.edu/study-finds-no-difference-in-the-amount-men-and-women-talk/.

128 **a great article in the *New York Times*** Kate Murphy, "You're Not Listening. Here's Why," *New York Times*, February 11, 2020, www.nytimes.com/2020/02/11/well/family/listening-relationships-marriage-closeness-communication-bias.html.

133 **Dan Sipp, an instructor who uses improv techniques** Dan Sipp, "How to Have Better Conversations," *The Holderness Family Podcast*, August 6, 2019, 5:00, hosted by Kim and Penn Holderness, podcast, MP3 audio, https://theholdernessfamily.com/conversations/.

141 **"we belong to one story / that the two, joining, made . . ."** Wendell Berry, "The Blue Robe," *New Collected Poems* (New York: Counterpoint Press, 2012), 315.

CHAPTER 9: I CHEATED ON YOU . . . FINANCIALLY

184 **guilt is when you feel bad** Brené Brown, "Shame v. Guilt," *Brené Brown* (blog), January 14, 2013, https://brenebrown.com/blog/2013/01/14/shame-v-guilt/.

185 **I define shame as** Brown.

CHAPTER 10: WHY ARE YOU BEING SO SNIPPY?

202 **the Monkey Business Illusion** Daniel Simons, "The Monkey Business Illusion," video shared by Daniel Simons, April 28, 2010, on YouTube, https://www.youtube.com/watch?v=IGQmdoK_ZfY.

ABOUT THE AUTHORS

Kim and Penn have been married for sixteen years. For seven of those years, they have chronicled their marriage and their family with funny music videos, vlogs, skits, and a podcast. Their videos have garnered over a billion views worldwide.

Penn and Kim honed their storytelling skills with twenty-five combined years in the TV news business. When the wonderful worlds of YouTube and Facebook appeared, Kim had the idea to ditch the traditional broadcast world and start making their own content in the digital space. Holderness Family Productions was born.

When they aren't dancing around like crazy people on your Facebook feed, Penn and Kim help international companies make videos of their own. They have produced and written content for StoryBots, Fox Home Entertainment, and most recently Velcro Companies, writing and directing a viral marketing campaign that landed their music video on *Anderson Cooper 360°*.

Interesting random facts about each of them:

- Kim was a competitive dancer growing up.
- Penn has weird thumbs that he can bend upside down.
- Kim was in a movie where she touched Robert Downey Jr. (*Iron Man 3*).
- Penn is an Eagle Scout.
- Kim dated the drummer from an eighties hair band.
- Penn really wants to go into space and reads books about orbital physics.
- Kim does not want Penn to go into space.

Penn and Kim live in Raleigh, North Carolina, with their children, Lola and Penn Charles. As of now, the kids love making silly videos with their parents.

For more Holderness family, visit
https://theholdernessfamily.com.